Henry VIII's
Health
in a Nutshell

Henry VIII's Health in a Nutshell

M
MadeGlobal Publishing

For more information on
MadeGlobal Publishing, visit our website:
www.madeglobal.com

Dedicated to Lewis Wayne Cornelius, my
wonderful father and a brilliant physician

Cover: Vintage Engraving of Henry VIII
from 1855

Contents

Figure 1 - Henry VIII from a vintage engraving from 1855

Introduction

Henry VIII is one of England's most well-known monarchs. Although he should be more justly famous for breaking England away from the Catholic church and creating the rough draft of the Church of England, it is the fact that he notoriously married six women and executed two of them during his desperate quest for a male heir that makes him stick in the public mind. Henry's popularity had led to many depictions of him in visual media and written fiction, showing him as everything from an uncouth, fat tyrant eating a turkey leg to a sexy and sex-crazed hound. Notwithstanding the imagined versions of him, Henry was more than an obese, reproductively challenged, marriage monger. In reality, the youthful king was athletic, intelligent and kind. It was only after his marriages and attempts at securing a male heir had gone spectacularly awry and his health had likewise failed that Henry turned into a monster.

The oddities of Henry's reign have inspired many people, laymen and historians alike, to postulate medical explanations for

his reproductive tribulations and his disintegrating health, both physically and mentally. Some theories try to explain why the king developed ulcers on his upper legs and became nearly immobile in his middle age. Other theories try to understand why the king who was once noted for his scholarship and chivalry became "a psychotic, paranoid bully" in his middle age[1]. A few theories try to formulate an answer for why Henry's reproductive track record is marred by foetal loss and neonatal deaths, and even fewer serve as an umbrella explanation for all the king's problems. His suspected ailments are legion, and harder to fit into a nutshell that one would expect.

One of the compounding factors about Henry's health is comorbidity. Any patient can have multiple illnesses at the same time, and the king was no exception. Considering the constellation of symptoms that hounded Henry, it is almost certain that he had more than a single ailment or underlying health issue. These myriad problems often overlap so that it is impossible to tell where one begins and the other ends without modern diagnostic tools. Lacking his DNA for analysis, all that scholars can offer is educated guesses and reasonable hypothesizes based on clues winkled out of historical record.

---

1   Hutchinson, page 209.

The worst legs in the world

One of the most simple and direct issues regarding Henry's health are the ulcerous legs that plagued him during the last third of his life. The suppurating lesions hurt as badly as they smelled. Henry must have hated them, not just because of the discomfort they caused him, but also because having weeping ulcers on his thighs was an assault on his vanity. Strong and unblemished legs were a necessity of male beauty in Henry's era, and having his handsomeness blighted by oozing abscesses doubtlessly wounded his pride. As a young man Henry had been openly conceited, with good cause, about his muscular limbs, bragging to a foreign ambassador that he had a "good calf to his leg". The sores must have been a constant reminder of the lost physique of his youth.

The theory that has the most medical and historical support is the premise that the king suffered from osteomyelitis[2]. Osteomyelitis is an infection of the bone, often caused by an injury. Henry probably injured the bones in his legs on one of the occasions when he fell

---

2   Ives, page 190.

Figure 2 - Detail of Henry VIII's legs from a portrait by the workshop of Hans Holbein the Younger

off his horse while hunting or jousting. Even if his femur hadn't been broken, a hairline fracture or a puncture on his leg could have created the conditions necessary for the bone to become diseased. Some of the symptoms of this kind of infection are bone pain; swelling which can show up in just a small, tender, inflamed spot or that can puff up the whole leg into a red, bloated agony-sausage; redness near the affected area; fever; nausea; chills; sweating and an overall impression that death would be a sweet mercy. Osteomyelitis can last the patient's whole life if not properly treated. When it is severe, the illness can cause tiny splinters of bone to separate from the femur and start migrating upward through the muscle and skin, creating suppurating ulcers. These sores are putridly smelly and grievously painful.

Another possibility is that Henry developed venous ulcers[3]. Venous skin ulcers are the result of poor blood circulation in the legs. Usually this is caused by venous insufficiency, when the one-way valves in your veins are damaged. The valves go only one-way in order to prevent blood from backwashing down the vein after every heartbeat, and if they can't do their job then the blood forms little pools that compromise the veins. This pooled blood may seep out of the unsound veins and flood the surrounding tissues. The saturated tissue can collapse and allow an open sore to form.

Venous leg ulcers are usually found on older patients who already have limited mobility, lack of physical exercise, high blood pressure, obesity, diabetes and varicose veins. Henry first developed a "sorre legge" in 1527 when he was only 36 and still very physically fit[4]. Other causal factors, such as smoking or working at a job that required him to stand for hours at a time, did not apply to the king. Venous ulcers also typically manifest below the knee, which does not fit the reoccurring ulcers on Henry's thighs.

---

3   Keynes, pages 180-1.
4   MacNalty

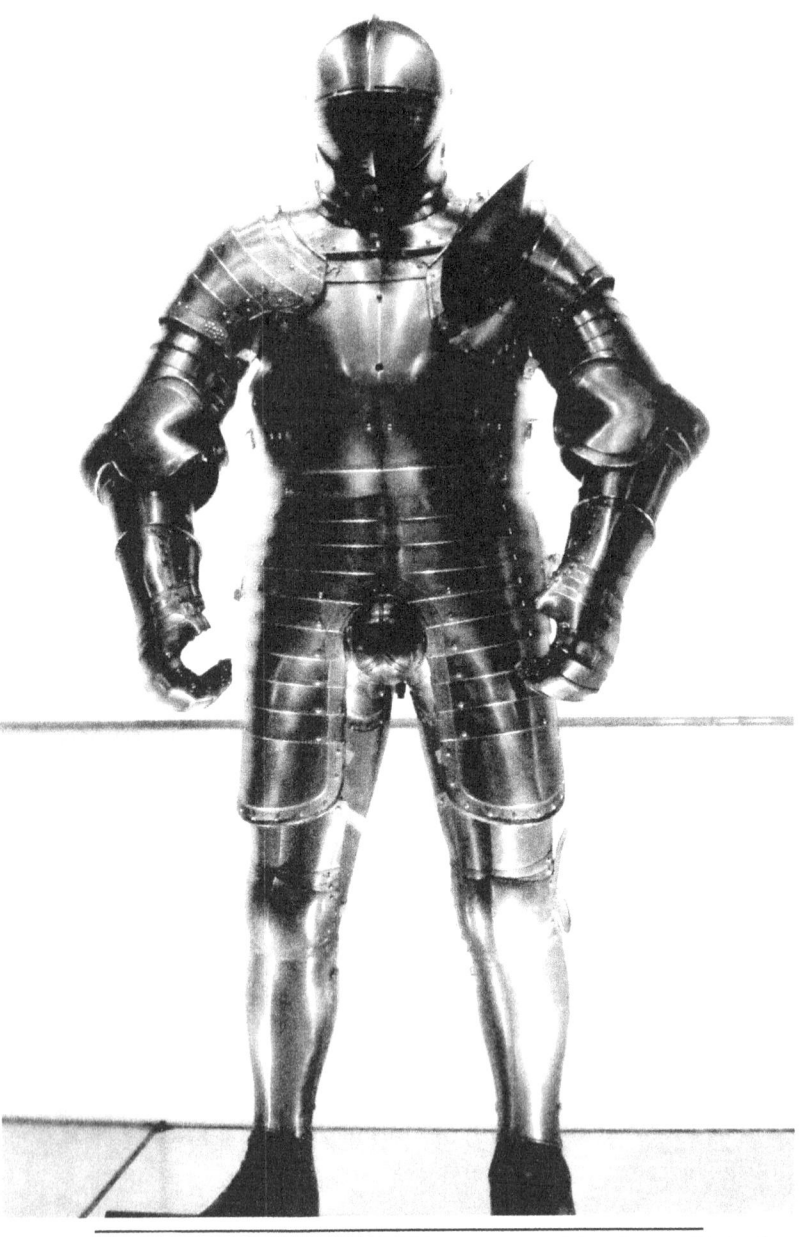

Figure 3 - Henry's May Day 1540 armour with a huge 51 inch
waist and 54.5 inch chest - Photo ©2012 Tim Ridgway

Although the ulcers on the king's thighs were more likely to have been osteomyelitis during the first decade that they bedevilled Henry, he may have later additionally developed venous ulcers on his upper leg due to complications of a deep vein thrombosis (DVT) following his jousting accident in 1536. The accident not only knocked him unconscious for more than two hours, it also crushed his legs when his horse landed on top of him. A crush injury can cause a blood clot in the deep veins of the legs even if none of the bones were broken or fractured and would have increased Henry's chances of developing venous ulcers[5].

In the 1540s, Henry began evincing ulcers below the knee that were more likely to have been caused by damaged veins than infected bones. Henry was also very fond of foods that were high in cholesterol, such as red meat, and dairy products, like cheese and butter. High levels of cholesterol in the blood (hypercholesterolemia) can exacerbate peripheral vascular disease. If Henry developed peripheral vascular disease, it "would seriously exacerbate venous ulceration, reducing the capacity for healing and causing difficulties in the fight against distal infection"[6]. Eating food fit for a king meant that Henry would have had a harder time healing and his ulcers would only grow worse.

The ulcers were not only unsightly and painful, they almost killed him. In the spring of 1538 one of the ulcers closed up, and seems to have loosened or created a blood clot that travelled to his lungs and caused a pulmonary embolism. Henry nearly died, and for more than a week he lay "black in the face without speaking"[7]. It is frankly a puzzle why he *didn't* shuffle off his mortal coil. A pulmonary embolism can easily kill a patient even now, despite the modern technological help of thrombolytic medicines and a surgical embolectomy. One of Henry's ulcers once again "suddenly closed to his great alarm" in March of 1541, terrifying him because

---

5   Chalmers and Chaloner
6   Chalmers and Chaloner
7   Park

"in the like case, he thought to have died"[8]. Fortunately for Henry, his physicians were somehow able to prevent a pulmonary embolism from occurring a second time.

Henry's legs were not only cankerous, they were also atrophying in some way. In May 1544, the imperial ambassador wrote that Henry had "the worst legs in the world, such that those who have seen them are astonished that he does not stay continually in bed", and that the king was "so very ill in his legs that it is a wonder he can stand"[9]. Henry's locomotion became so severely limited that he had two custom chairs, referred to as "trams", made so he could be carried throughout the palace and he "could not go up or down stairs unless he was raised up or let down by an engine"[10].

It has been argued that the king's enormous bulk was the source of his immobility, not any kind of muscular wasting. Thanks to his "marvelous excess" at the table, Henry had grown increasingly fat. His waist measured 54" in 1541[11]. Nevertheless, that did not mean he was too fat to walk. Even morbidly obese people who are more than 200lb (90kg) overweight are usually still ambulatory, so his weight alone would not explain his lessened ability to traverse. Furthermore, the muscular weakness Henry experienced appears to have been worse in his lower limbs. At the age of 44, Henry was still healthy and strong enough to ride and hunt, in spite of his weight, but he needed a "hoist" to successfully mount his horse[12]. He would have required another underlying medical condition, one that centred on his lower limbs in particular, to have compromised his mobility to such an extent without impairing his ability to ride. Rather than Henry's weight affecting his ability to move, the reverse might be true. The king did not attain truly gargantuan proportions until after he was bedridden and unable to ride any

---

8   CSP, Vol 16, 3 March 1541.
9   CSP, Vol. 19 Part 1, 18 May 1544.
10   Ackroyd, page 176.
11   Erickson, page 328.
12   Chalmers and Chaloner.

longer. His chronic incapacitation from muscular atrophy may have been the reason why Henry weighed just shy of 400lb (180kg) at the time of his death[13].

Gout is sometimes proffered as an explanation of Henry's attenuated legs, but upon closer examination the theory is also seen to be weak. In most cases, gout causes "kidney stones in its victims and painful swelling of the big toe, the latter so common as to be almost synonymous with the disease"[14], but Henry never exhibited either of those symptoms. If there had been any sign of gout, the royal physicians would have certainly diagnosed it. Remedies for gout had been part of Western medical training since Dioscorides and Pliny the Elder 1,500 years before. Often it is assumed that Henry must have been gouty, simply because he was overweight. This is an incorrect assumption, since there is no correlation between gout and obesity except in old wives' tales.

Type II diabetes is also postulated to have been the outcome of Henry's tremendous adipose tissue gain, but the link between fat and type II diabetes is as tenuous as that between obesity and gout. This is probably a shock to most people, since the correlation is implied in almost every media report about type II diabetes or the obesity epidemic, but in reality almost half of all type II diabetes sufferers are of normal weight and the large majority of obese people will *never* develop the disease. Type II diabetes occurs when the body can no longer process insulin correctly, and is a metabolic disease that can strike whatever the patient's weight. Genetics and poverty rather than weight or diet seems to be the biggest factor. Some ethnicities, such as Hispanic/Latino Americans, African-Americans, Native Americans, Asian-Americans, Pacific Islanders and Alaska natives, all have higher risks of developing type II diabetes. Being poor also increases the risk, even when ALL other factors – including weight – are taken into account. Nevertheless,

---

13   Chalmers and Chaloner.
14   Park, page 38.

obesity and type II diabetes are so often studied *together* that general misinformation linking them remains strong even in the medical community.

What *can* be correlated to both obesity and diabetes is a sedentary lifestyle. Sitting at work and then coming home and sitting some more "were both associated with significantly increased risk of diabetes in multivariate analyses adjusting for dietary and nondietary covariates"[15]. Basically, sitting down too much is a bigger risk to your health than almost anything else, including what you eat and what you weigh.

Ironically, Henry's weight might have been a health *advantage*. Type II diabetes is yet another illness that experiences what researchers call the "obesity paradox". Rather than hurting the patient, excess adipose increases survival rates. Overweight and obese people with type II diabetes *live longer than* normal or underweight people diagnosed with the same illness. Henry's large body mass may have initially aided his longevity, contrary to common belief.

Occasionally it is suggested that type II diabetes is the explanation for Henry's problematic reproduction and mental alterations, as well as for his leg ulcers. If Henry had type II diabetes, then it might provide an explanation for his personality change, infertility and ill health after midlife, but would not address the reproductive problems that tormented his first two wives. The suggested link between fertility problems and diabetes in his early reproductive history is highly unlikely. Miscarriage due to diabetes is typically linked to the mother having diabetes, not the father. Although superstructure defects in the sperm of male diabetics can increase the chances of a miscarriage in their partners, these miscarriages would occur early in the first trimester because the embryo would be nonviable. The more common side-effects of diabetes are erectile

---

15   Hu et al.

dysfunction and low sperm count, which could explain the lack of pregnancies in his marriages to his fifth and sixth wives, but could not account for the frequent pregnancies and subsequent late-term miscarriages experienced by his first two queens.

Near the end of Henry's life, yet another problem developed in his legs – they became grotesquely swollen. The most likely cause of this swelling was congestive heart failure. The king was a corpulent invalid and his blood pressure was unlikely to still be in the normal range later in his life. Hypertension would have promoted the retention of fluid in his legs and ankles, intensifying his immobility and weight. The less he moved, the worse his blood pressure would have become. Henry's sedentary existence would have subsequently encouraged the development of type II diabetes, which would have caused attendant venous ulcers and depression, which would in turn have made it harder for Henry to move or exercise[16]. Henry would thus have become trapped in a perpetual circle of worsened health until, wherein his ailments fed and sustained one another in a kind of perfect storm that only ended with his death in January 1547.[17]

---

16   Hu; Katon et al.
17   Other theories regarding Henry's health try to account for his ulcerated and devitalized limbs, but since those theories focus mainly on trying to answer questions regarding his pursuit of a male heir and his volatile change in personality, they appear in those sections of the book.

A brief account of
the king's offspring

When Henry married Katherina of Aragon, often spelt Catherine, on 11 June 1509, everyone was hopeful that the newlyweds would have their first child, preferably a son and heir, quickly. Things seemed promising. The new bride felt her first known pregnancy quicken in November, just five months after the wedding. Sadly, the joy was short-lived. Katherina prematurely gave birth to a stillborn girl on 31 January 1510. Her loss was kept strictly secret with only a handful of trusted attendants and healers in the know. Women who miscarried were open to speculation that they had offended God or practised witchcraft, and her friends were eager to protect their beloved and long-suffering queen from malicious gossip. To add a complication, after the delivery her uterus swelled so much that physicians thought there might be another, still living, foetus inside. This was a real possibility, so the doctor wasn't being unreasonable to suggest it. Regretfully, the physician was wrong in this case. The king was told that Katherina was still pregnant and was due to give birth in May. In April, the queen retired for her lying-in, a month before the expected birth. This she would spend lying in bed in a dimly lit room with only women as her attendants. It was only when May arrived with no baby to be seen that Henry was told of her prior miscarriage.

Luckily for Katherina, she conceived again almost immediately, some time in late April or early May, meaning that Henry was clearly visiting his wife when she was in confinement. This is not as *outré* as it would seem to those who know about the medieval belief that pregnant women should not have sex. It was a bit more complicated than that. Although the "rules" about sex during pregnancy discouraged intercourse in some months in a woman's pregnancy, medical wisdom *encouraged* coitus during other months of the gravid period. One of the months in which sex was encouraged was the final month of pregnancy, because it was thought that the father could "fashion" his child and "set his influence on it" by engaging in sexual activity with the mother at this time[18]. If both Henry and Katherina believed, based on the doctor's speculations, that there was a growing foetus in her womb, they would have thought it both prudent and pleasurable to engage in frequent sexual intercourse during her lying-in. The king was still in his teens and doubtlessly had a strong sex drive, so this would probably not have been a hardship for him.

Two pregnancies in rapid succession demonstrate fairly conclusively that both she and Henry were fertile together. On New Year's Day 1511, she had a son, the new Prince of Wales, who they named Henry after his father. He initially seemed to be a healthy baby and the entire kingdom was in a state of celebration. Tragically, the infant prince died on 22 February 1511. In September of the same year it was rumoured that the queen might be pregnant again, but that hope seems to have come to naught. This may be

18   Cressy, page 46.

indicative of either an erroneous wish or an early, unreported miscarriage.

Owing to Henry's absence for military reasons, she did not conceive again until 1513. In October of that year she had a premature son who died shortly after his birth, to her great grief and regret. Katherina's sorrows continued when in November 1514, she gave birth to yet another son who died within hours. Finally, on 18 February 1516, she had a healthy daughter, Mary. This baby girl would later rule England as Mary I and receive the rather unfair nickname "Bloody Mary" for her draconian yet sincere attempts to deter the Protestant movement. Katherina was possibly pregnant again in August 1517, but it was never officially announced. Her final acknowledged pregnancy ended in November 1518, when she gave birth to a baby girl who died shortly thereafter. She had a total of six official and perhaps two unofficial pregnancies, but only one surviving child.

Much to Katherina's humiliation and distress, Henry had a healthy son by his mistress, Bessie Blount, in 1519. It was Bessie's first pregnancy, but possibly not her only child by the king. Some historians believe she presented him with a girl a few years later. If so, the king never acknowledged Bessie's daughter as he had done their son, who he named Henry Fitzroy and heaped with honours. Henry Fitzroy was healthy as an infant and throughout childhood, but he became ill and died of unknown causes in 1536 when he was just 17 years old.

Henry had ceased having sexual relations with Katherina by 1524, and he sought to nullify the marriage on the grounds that a passage in Leviticus forbids a man to marry his brother's widow. Some scholars argue that it was around this time that Henry had an affair with Mary Boleyn that resulted in two children, but the historical consensus is that the affair was real but the children were not his[19].

---

19   Licence

Henry's desire to end his first marriage had intensified by 1527. Not only did he want to remarry in the hopes of having a son, he had also fallen in love with Anne Boleyn, the younger sister of his former mistress Mary Boleyn. Henry eventually tired of petitioning Rome to nullify his first union, and to expedite matters, declared himself head of the Church of England and had the Archbishop of Canterbury dissolve his marriage to Katherina. Henry and Anne Boleyn were secretly married in November 1532, then again on 25 January 1533. Anne was crowned queen in May of that same year, and in September her first and only child, Elizabeth, was born. The infant princess, later to become Elizabeth I and one of England's greatest rulers, was healthy and strong. Although Henry would have preferred a boy, as did everyone at the time, he was sanguine that a healthy first baby presaged more children for himself and Anne.

The king seemed to be right in his prediction of their future fertility when his wife was visibly pregnant again in January 1534. Anne was due around the end of July, but some time in late June she went into premature labour. The baby was either stillborn or died shortly after birth, and its sex was left unreported. The king and queen never made an official announcement about the end of the pregnancy, and it is possible that Anne had a phantom pregnancy. Again, the queen may have had an early miscarriage in September of 1534, but it was never reported as an official pregnancy and the existence of the pregnancy is a topic of historical debate. She may have been pregnant once more in March of 1535 and experienced a miscarriage near the end of her second trimester, but that pregnancy is likewise debated. Her final undisputed pregnancy ended calamitously when she miscarried a boy in January 1536. She seems to have been shortly into the second trimester when the foetus spontaneously aborted. In April she was accused of adultery and treason and, after a brief trial in a kangaroo court, was beheaded on 19 May 1536.

Henry married Jane Seymour on 30 May 1536, and their son, Edward, was born on 12 October 1537. Sadly, Jane died of puerperal fever, commonly called childbed fever, just twelve days later. The new Prince of Wales, who would later ascend the throne as Edward VI in 1547, was Henry's fourth and final child to survive infancy. None of Henry's subsequent marriages, or mistresses, ever gave him more *known* offspring. Without some form of confirmation about royal paternity, his reputed children must be excluded from the list of his progeny.

Thus, the king fathered a total of at least eleven, and possibly sixteen, pregnancies with four different women. Fertility was obviously not Henry's problem. It was foetal and neonate mortality that denied him his heirs.[20]

Several theories have been proffered to explain the extreme foetal and neonate mortality of Henry's offspring, but these frequently centre on possible ailments experienced by the king's wives. There are a few postulations regarding Henry's losses that look at the king's physiology for answers. The best known of these is the speculation that Henry had syphilis. However, a theory from 2010 regarding Henry's blood antigens has also been gaining ground in academic and public forums, and unlike the idea that the king had syphilis, it has not been disproven.

---

20   It is impossible to know for certain how many times Henry's reproductive partners may have actually conceived. Considering the fact that poor nutrition, even for the wealthiest women, made it likely that irregular periods were not uncommon, simply missing a menstrual period or having a longer interval between menses would not have been seen as anything other than a hopeful sign of possible conception. Pregnancies were often well into the second trimester before they would be reported, since women of that time did not consider themselves to be truly pregnant until the foetus "quickened", i.e. the mother could feel movement in her uterus. Quickening was so crucial because it was assumed that until the foetus could be felt moving that it did not have a soul and was therefore not really a person, or even necessarily alive (Ginsburg, 1989; Fraser, 1992). Therefore, Henry's reproductive partners could have easily had miscarriages in the first trimester of pregnancy that were unknown and, thus, unreported.

The idea that king had syphilis was first postulated by a Victorian physician in 1888[21]. Since the Victorians viewed Henry as a rotter, a bounder and a rascal, as well as believing venereal disease to be the due punishment from God for having sex outside the confines of holy matrimony, this hypothesis was more or less accepted as an enjoyably lewd certainty for the next few decades. The theory was soundly and conclusively debunked in 1931 by Frederik Chamberlin, but that didn't halt the spread of the salacious slander. The premise that Henry was riddled with syphilis was just too delightfully raunchy to refute. Even now, 100 years after it was unmasked as a myth, the idea that the king had this particular sexually transmitted disease keeps re-emerging from the depths of social media.

The fact is that neither Henry nor any of his wives ever showed symptoms of syphilis. Henry lived long enough that the tertiary stage of syphilis, which usually appears within three to ten years of contracting the disease, would have developed. This stage of syphilis is hard to overlook. It results in gaping sores in the lymph node areas, potentially the destruction of the nasal cavity, loss of the front teeth and palate erosion, and granulomatous lesions -- especially on the scalp and tibia. It would be extremely unlikely that syphilis would manifest as sores on Henry's thighs for twenty-plus years but show no other symptoms. In a court setting wherein Henry was attended at the bath and toilet by courtiers, the physical signs of syphilis would not have been unnoted. More to the point, the physicians of Henry's time were aware of the nature of the syphilitic symptoms. If they had seen signs of the "Great Pox" on the king, they would have identified his symptoms as such and attempted to treat him accordingly.[22] The most common treatment

---

21   Keynes, page 179.
22   Contrary to the popular misconception that syphilis was brought to Europe
      by Columbus when he returned from North America, there is convincing
      archaeological evidence of skeletons exhumed from medieval London graveyards
      that predate 1493, which display tertiary syphilis (Glass, 2001).

for syphilis by Tudor physicians involved dosing syphilitic patients with massive quantities of mercury, yet Henry was never given mercury[23] nor any other putative cure.

Furthermore, it does not solve the mystery of the death of Henry's neonates and foetuses. Syphilis can only cause miscarriage if the mother has the disease or if the foetus has been exposed during pregnancy. Even then, children with congenital syphilis often survive infancy, in spite of cognitive and physical handicaps. Some people argue that three of his surviving children were the first born in Henry's new relationship with their mothers, and therefore the women may not have contracted syphilis from him early enough for it to have affected their firstborn children. However, this argument cannot be made in relation to his daughter Mary. If Henry had been syphilitic then Mary Tudor would have almost certainly been affected in light of the fact that she was the fifth born child of his first wife, Katherina of Aragon. If syphilis was to blame as the cause of the many miscarriages preceding Mary's birth, then her mother would have become infected almost immediately after her marriage to the king. In addition, none of Henry's four surviving children showed symptoms consistent with congenital syphilis as adults. Although both his sons died in their teens, their health problems more closely resembled tuberculosis than any other known disease at the time. Furthermore, typical manifestations of congenital syphilis include an alteration to the teeth referred to as Hutchinson's incisors and mulberry molars, as well as rashes and skin infections resembling secondary syphilis occurring within the first few weeks of life[24]. None of these ailments or problems was reported in any of Henry's offspring.

The latest theory that attempts to formulate a reason for Henry's reproductive disappointments and mental alteration as an older king is the postulation that Henry had a Kell positive

---

23   Fraser, page 335.
24   Cunningham et. al.; Larsen

blood type, and that he developed the McLeod syndrome as a consequence[25]. Henry's Kell positive blood type would explain why his sexual partners suffered foetal and neonatal loss, while McLeod's syndrome would explain why the king became physically weaker and mentally unstable in his later years.

The Kell antigen system is determined by a group of antigens on the human red blood cells and most individuals are negative for the antibody system. If Henry had a Kell positive blood type and his sexual partner did not, then any Kell positive foetus conceived after the first pregnancy would be attacked by the mother's antibodies. After giving birth to the first Kell positive infant, or miscarrying a Kell positive foetus at any time during the pregnancy, a small amount of blood from the embryo will have been transferred to the mother. This blood transfer will cause her to experience alloimmunization, and therefore develop anti-Kell antibodies. The mother will now be "allergic" to any Kell positive foetus in her womb, and her subsequent Kell positive pregnancies are at risk because her antibodies will attack the foetus as though it were a dangerous foreign body, such as a virus. Foetuses that are Kell negative will not be attacked by the mother's antibodies, and will thus carry to term if otherwise healthy. Therefore, being Kell positive is only a reproductive problem if the *father* of the foetus has the Kell antigens, since a mother who is Kell positive will not have an alloimmunization to either Kell positive or Kell negative foetuses.

When a Kell negative mother's body attacks a Kell positive foetus it usually results in an illness know as haemolytic disease of the new-born (HDN), which is also called foetal erythroblastosis. HDN happens when the mother's antibodies have destroyed the baby's red blood cells. In milder cases, this attack on the infant's red blood cells will just cause anaemia, where there will be too few red blood cells but not to the point where it is fatal, and/or jaundice

25   Whitley and Kramer

when the red blood cells break down and produce bilirubin which can turn the baby yellow but usually isn't a serious problem. During HDN, the baby's red blood cells are attacked in mass quantities by the mother's antibodies, which leads to hydrops foetalis, where fluid starts to build up in the abdomen, heart and lungs and which places pressure on the heart. This affects the hearts ability to pump. There can also be autoimmune haemolytic anaemia where so many red blood cells burst that there is insufficient blood plasma. The foetal response to maternal anti-Kell antibodies is the second most common reason for HDN[26]. HDN and its complications are incredibly dangerous now and would have been almost uniformly fatal to a new-born in the Tudor era.

Because of the alloimmunization, a Kell negative woman carrying a Kell positive foetus often results in the pregnancy naturally aborting some time after twenty weeks gestation. Some pregnancies do result in infants born between thirty-one to forty weeks, but without modern medical intervention those babies will also usually die within twenty-four hours of birth[27]. This means that a Kell negative woman whose partner is a Kell positive man has an increased risk of suffering from repeated late-term miscarriages, stillbirths and the death of her new-borns shortly after they are delivered[28]. More rarely, infants can have hypo regenerative anaemia, which is basically the manifestation of HDN being delayed, in which case symptoms do not appear until two to six weeks after birth and therefore the baby may not die until it is a month or two old[29]. The obstetrical losses suffered by Henry's first two queens are similar to, and in some cases identical to, documented cases of Kell affected pregnancies[30].

---

26 Sanguinis; Marsh and Redman; Berkowtiz et al; Caine and Meuller-Heubach; Baichoo and Bruce-Tageo; Mayne et al; Goh, et al; Bowman, et al; Win et al
27 Baichoo and Bruce-Tafgoe
28 Santiago, et al
29 Luban
30 Whitley and Kramer

Since most people with the Kell positive blood type can pass either a Kell positive or a Kell negative gene on to their children, every pregnancy fathered by Henry had roughly a fifty/fifty chance of being Kell negative. Any Kell positive foetus conceived after the first birth would have initiated a deadly alloimmunization within the mother's womb, but a Kell negative foetus would not be attacked by the mother's antibodies and would have as much chance of survival as any other healthy baby born during this era. This explains why at least one of his children, Mary, survived even though she was not the first-born of Katherina of Aragon. If Mary, the fifth baby born to Henry's first queen, did not get the Kell positive gene from her father then she would have been safe in the womb, unlike her Kell positive siblings.[31] The pregnancies of Henry's second queen, Anne Boleyn, were a textbook example of a healthy first child and subsequent late-term miscarriages. Any of Anne's pregnancies conceived after the birth of her daughter, Elizabeth, had unsuccessful outcomes. Henry's third queen, Jane Seymour, had only one child before her death, but a healthy firstborn is normal with a Kell positive father. The only mistress formally acknowledged to have given Henry a child was Bessie Blount, who produced a healthy firstborn son, but then had no more children by the king.

Problems in pregnancy due to a Kell positive foetus are uncommon, but men with Kell positive blood are not necessarily rare. An American study that took place between 1993 and 1995 found that 22% of the women surveyed with a positive antibody screen had antibodies that would attack a foetus will the Kell positive blood type[32]. In England approximately 9% of the population has

---

31   Katherina's second child, the New Year's boy, died at less than two months old but his death does not have any characteristics that mark it as Kell related HDN. It is likely that the baby boy was Kell negative, like Mary, and his death was the result of one of the myriad common illnesses that killed infants during this period of history.

32   Geifman-Holtzman

a blood type positive for the Kell antigen[33]. Nevertheless, the small percentage of Kell positive people means that 91% of Henry's potential queens were Kell negative. Such numbers suggest that the frequency of this blood group in England is common enough that it would be a reasonable explanation for Henry's reproductive problems.

While the theory that Henry VIII was Kell positive is based primarily on the fact that the reproductive patterns of his partners are consistent with that of a Kell positive father, there is nevertheless at least one other source that provides evidence for the theory: Henry's family tree. In family trees carrying the Kell positive gene the daughters are able to reproduce successfully but male lines tend to die out. This is precisely what occurred in the offspring of Henry's maternal great-grandmother, Jacquetta Woodville.

Jacquetta of Luxembourg came to England to marry royalty but fell in love with and married Richard Woodville, a mere earl, after she was widowed. It was all very scandalous at the time. She and Richard had fourteen children, and all but one of them lived to adulthood. Her daughters were all able to reproduce, but Jacquetta's sons were mostly childless. Henry VIII's mother was one of Jacquetta's granddaughters, and Henry's maternal cousins descended from his Woodville grandmother had similar reproductive troubles to his own.

In their 2013 article in the *Journal of Royal College of Physicians of Edinburgh*[34], doctors Stride and Lopes-Floro argued that the reproductive patterns of Jacquetta's sons are:

> [C]learly relevant in establishing whether she could have been a carrier of the Kell positive gene. As previously noted, K/k homozygosity is rare, and it is more probable that Jacquetta could have been a K/k heterozygote, such that her offspring had a 50%

---

33   Mayne et al
34   Journal of Royal College of Physicians of Edinburgh 43, 4 pages 353-360.

chance of inheriting the immunogenic K allele. If this is correct we would expect to find that a review of her Kell positive male children would have not more than a single healthy child. Lewis Woodville, the first son, born in 1438, appears from limited information to have died age 12 in 1451 without issue. Anthony Woodville, the second son, born in 1442, played a leading role in the events of the time; he was an excellent jouster, and fought in the battles of Towton and Barnet. Though twice married he never had any children. John Woodville, the third son, born in 1445, was married to Catherine Neville, the Dowager Duchess of Norfolk, a marriage of political expediency perhaps to advance the power of the Woodville family. She was at least 65 years old, he was 19 or 20, yet she outlived him, as John was executed in 1469. Unsurprisingly there were no children. Lionel Woodville, the fourth son, born in 1447, went into the church, becoming Bishop of Salisbury. There is no evidence of marriage or offspring, beyond improbable rumours that he fathered Stephen Gardiner, subsequent Bishop of Winchester. Lionel is recorded as being the first person to receive an honorary university degree, in this case from Oxford. Richard Woodville, the fifth son, officially did not marry, and had no children. Richard adopted a low profile and tried to avoid taking sides in the War of the Roses. There are unconfirmed rumours that he married secretly and had one son, who was raised under a different name to avoid the violent deaths of many of his relatives. Edward Woodville, the sixth son, born in 1455, appears never to have married and had no known children. Thomas Woodville, the seventh son, is documented as marrying Ann Holland, but history does not record any offspring. Thus of seven sons, four clearly had no children, and the other three had no documented offspring. Only Anthony and Thomas had documented marriages, but no children; Lewis died young; John married a postmenopausal woman; and Lionel, Richard and Edward never married. This does not confirm or refute Kell blood group positivity, but it supports the above deduction that Jacquetta was the most likely source of this condition if it is causative. As such, Jacquetta's genes may well have been the curse preventing Henry VIII's attempts to produce healthy male heirs.

The reproductive record of Henry and his partners, in conjunction with the reproductive issues shown in Henry's maternal lineage, lend strong evidence to the idea that the king had a Kell positive blood type. Due to the fact that none of Henry's children had offspring of their own, it is impossible to gather further evidence by following the Kell positive gene reproductive pattern via Henry's direct descendants.

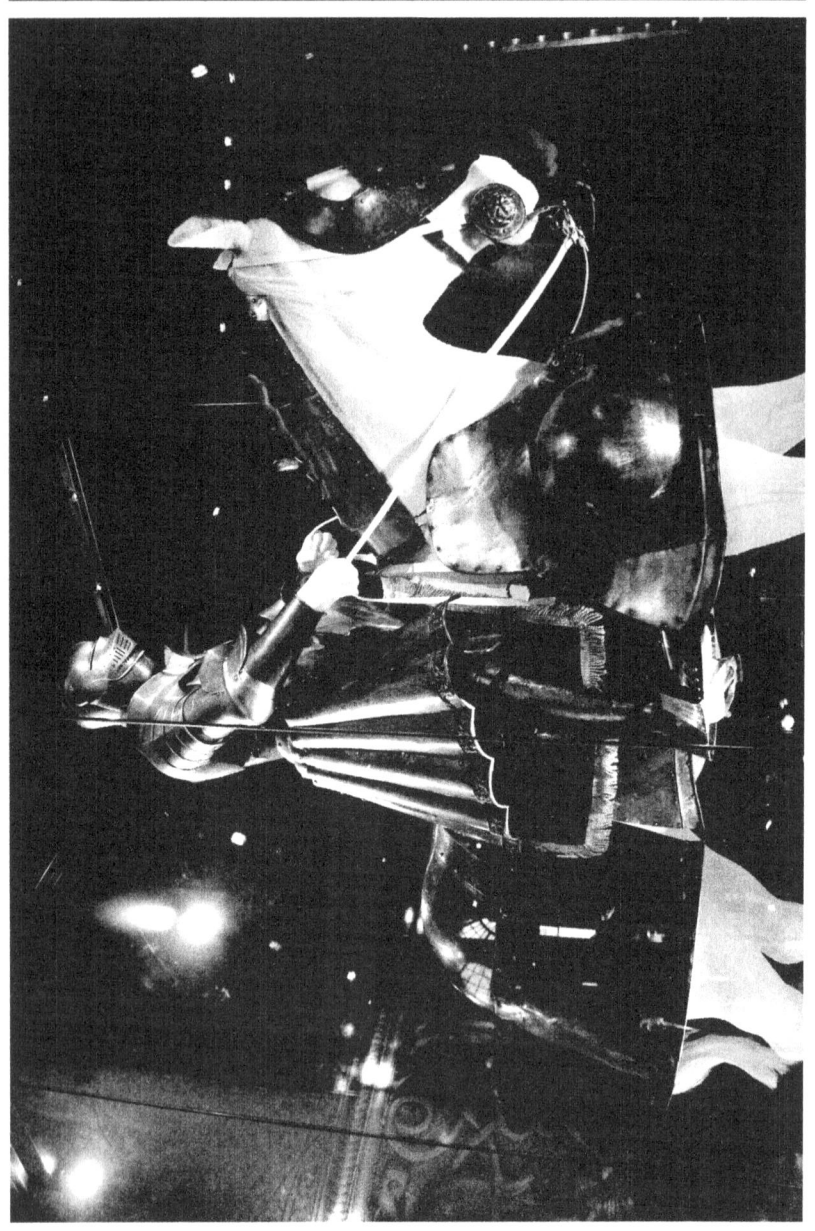

Figure 4 - Henry's famous "Silvered and Engraved" armour, made around 1515 - Photo ©2012 Tim Ridgway

A tale of two Henrys:
The king before and after 1531

How much did Henry actually change? Isn't it an exaggeration to imply he was a radically different person after his fortieth birthday?

No.

When he was a child, Henry was visited by Erasmus of Rotterdam, a humanist who was esteemed as "the most celebrated scholar of his age"[35], and Erasmus was so impressed by the future monarch's intellectual abilities that he called Henry "a universal genius". This was a fairly accurate assessment. Along with many other interests, Henry was educated in mathematics, the sciences, engineering, astronomy, cartography and was acknowledged as a musical prodigy. He was also fluent in French and Latin, as well as having a good command of Italian and Spanish.

---

35   Erickson, page 27.

Figure 5 - Portrait of Henry VIII by the workshop of
Hans Holbein the Younger

Not only was Henry mentally gifted, the gods favoured him physically as well. His skeleton, which was exhumed in 1813, proved that he was 6'2" – immensely tall for his time period. His historical armour measurements that were taken in 1514, when he was a young man of 23, record that he had a 35" waist and a 42" chest. In today's terms, this means he would be the same height and have roughly the same bodily demotions as Will Smith had when he starred in the 2007 movie *I Am Legend*. The personal correspondence of first-hand witness in the spring of 1515 described Henry as "the handsomest potentate I ever set eyes on; above the usual height, with an extremely fine calf to his leg, his complexion very fair and bright, with auburn hair combed straight and short, in the French fashion, and a round face so very beautiful that it would become a pretty woman"[36]. Henry's muscles weren't just for show – he was a magnificent athlete who could ride for hours and he played almost every sport and game well. He was also more of a warrior than people realize, and was as good in the martial sports as he was in those with less serious intent. The king could draw "the bow with greater strength than any man in England", and was said to have jousted "marvelously"[37].

Henry was certainly not a saint as a youth, but his only significant personality flaws seem to be egocentricity and a propensity to show off. That he was a bit full of himself is not surprising, since he was a polymath sports hero who had been taught since birth to believe that he was, *literally*, second only to God.[38] Henry was a devout Catholic and somewhat ridged theologically, but he nevertheless enjoyed debates on the topic of faith and would listen to opinions that differed from his own with "remarkable courtesy and unruffled

---

36   CSP Vol. 2 pages 104-118.
37   CSP Vol.2, pages 104-118.
38   During the Tudor period it was commonly believed that the king was anointed by God, and therefore any person who acted against Henry also acted against God

temper"[39]. In contrast, as an older man Henry was inclined to execute those who disagreed with him.

Henry, who would later be characterized by his implacable wrath, was thought of as a very reasonable man during his earlier reign. His personal physician described the young king as "cheerful and gamesome"[40]. William Blount, the 4th Baron Mountjoy, who was an acclaimed humanist and knew the young king well, could not praise Henry enough. Mountjoy wrote to Erasmus of "how nobly, how wisely, the prince behaves", and that the whole of England was "in ecstasies"[41] to have such a monarch, as well as declaring that:

> I have no fear but when you heard that our Prince, now Henry the Eighth, whom we may call our Octavius, had succeeded to his father's throne, all your melancholy left you at once. What may you not promise yourself from a Prince with whose extraordinary and almost Divine character you are acquainted? When you know what a hero he now shows himself, how wisely he behaves, what a lover he is of justice and goodness, what affection he bears to the learned I will venture to swear that you will need no wings to make you fly to behold this new and auspicious star. Oh, my Erasmus, if you could see how all the world here is rejoicing in the possession of so great a prince, how his life is all their desire, you could not contain your tears for joy.[42]

An older Henry would go on to judicially murder Mountjoy's grandson on Tower Hill on 9 December 1538 for the iniquitous crime of being too closely related to the throne. There was neither

---

39   CSP Vol 4, pages 2376-2385.
40   Erickson, page 283.
41   CSP Vol 1, pages 24-34.
42   Lacey

justice nor goodness in the act, and it is a small mercy that Mountjoy was no longer alive to see Henry's egregious behaviour.

Henry was also loyal and compassionate in his youth. When he married Katherina of Aragon in 1509 he was marrying an impoverished window who had nothing substantial to offer either politically or financially. Katherina's royal father had shown himself to care little for his daughter's fate, and she had long since been reduced to selling personal jewellery to buy household supplies and clothes. Worse, she was widow of the king's brother and the possibility that she consummated her first marriage could overshadow their union. She was attractive, but not so great a beauty that a king would throw himself away on her. The Spanish ambassador was so certain Henry wouldn't marry her that he had "already ordered Katherina's belongings packed when news of the planned marriage reached him"[43]. As a boy, the king had written Katherina letters that assured her that he loved her and he had promised to marry her, and he remembered his pledge and kept his word. Instead of leaving her a financially and emotionally distressed widow, and taking the more prudent course of seeking a richer and more influential bride, Henry chivalrously wed Katherina shortly after he became king.

The king was one of the more faithful monarchs in Europe. His affairs were extremely discrete, the sixteenth century's version of royal fidelity. Unlike other monarchs, Henry did not appoint official mistresses or flaunt them in the queen's face. Neither was he in constant pursuit of the next paramour. Henry tended to confine his affairs to times when the queen was pregnant and could not have intercourse for months at a stretch. Like most men of his time, the king believed that if his wife wasn't readily available to him then it was perfectly permissible for him to relieve his sexual needs with other women. Considering that Henry could have been utterly profligate with no recourse for Katherina except to bear it,

---

43   Erickson, page 53.

HISTORY "In a Nutshell" SERIES

he was moderation and chastity personified. His motto was Sir Loyal Heart and, until the radical personality change that occurred in the middle of his affair with Anne Boleyn, he was always careful to keep his liaisons subdued. He made every effort to prevent his infidelities from being a source of humiliation to Katherina and he never put another woman ahead of her, either in public or in private. It is said of Henry that he was the only king to have more wives than mistresses, and "by the standards of his time he was positively uxorious"[44].

His relative fidelity was even more remarkable considering how often ambitious courtiers waved their pretty young female relations under Henry's nose as tempting bait. Cardinal Wolsey, who as the Lord Chancellor practically controlled the English government on Henry's behalf until the 1530s, was accused of acting as "the King's bawd", a panderer who guaranteed the king his choice of women who "were most wholesome and with the best complexions"[45]. Even if the accusations against Wolsey were untrue, there were plenty of other men at court who paraded female kindred before the king in the hopes she could secure his affections. Male family members of the king's inamoratas could expect to turn the women's favours into political and financial favours, since almost invariably the family of the king's mistress would receive such lagniappe as court positions, titles and lands. Even without the pressure of familial ambitions and the incentive of receiving royal gratuities, women probably would have been attracted to Henry because of his good looks and athleticism. When these facts are taken into consideration, it is plain that he was loyal to his wife far beyond what was expected of him by the cultural standards of his day.

So it was that Henry began his reign as an attractive, affable teenager who was respected as one of the most learned men in Europe. It is no wonder that Thomas More, who the older Henry

---

44   Fraser, page 220.
45   Matusiak

would later execute, described the younger Henry as "the everlasting glory" of his time[46]. Yet the average person is mostly familiar with the middle-aged, corpulent Henry who had the obnoxious habit of executing his wives. The moderate, loyal, loving, intelligent and rational king became a brutal, bloodthirsty, paranoid bully in his forties, a brute who "never spared a man in his anger nor a woman in his lust"[47].

Some historians blame the pain in his legs for the fact he grew so emotionally unstable and outright cruel in his forties. Notwithstanding the ill-temper pain can bring, it may not have been pain alone that was causing Henry to become cantankerous. There is substantial evidence that Henry underwent a significant change in his personality and mental perspicacity that cannot be correlated with the agony in his limbs. For one thing, Henry's mental changes seem to have occurred with devastating swiftness long after his legs were causing him to suffer. In 1527, Henry's legs were already ulcerated, but when Thomas More told Henry he believed that the king's marriage to Katherina of Aragon was valid the king never threatened More to attempt to change his opinion. It was only half a dozen or so years later, in 1534, that the king turned against More and had him imprisoned. The following year Henry executed the renowned scholar, an action that sent a "shock wave that went out across Europe"[48]. More's death was a particularly pointless and unreasonable act considering the fact that he had accepted Henry's marriage to Anne Boleyn, assuring the king that he would not "murmur at it nor dispute upon it"[49]. Henry, when faced with universal disapproval for this unjust execution, threw Anne Boleyn to the wolves and blamed her for his decision to kill More.

---

46   Robinson, page 37.
47   Ward
48   Erickson, page 257.
49   Fraser, page 190.

The worst thing the king seemed capable of before 1531 was gross hypocrisy. For example, even though Henry was in the midst of a nullity suit against Katherina while simultaneously wooing Anne Boleyn, he took the time to chastise his sister, Margaret, for her attempt to divorce her husband, the Earl of Angus. Unlike Henry, Margaret had grounds for her divorce that were commonly accepted as reasons to void a marriage. The earl had been precontracted to marry another woman. In spite of the fact that his sister had a much more secure religious and legal rational to end her marriage than he did, Henry wrote to Margaret instructing her that she should respect the "divine ordinance of inseparable matrimony", and reminded her of the "danger of damnation" to which she was subjecting herself[50]. Although this shows him to be impervious to irony, it is not irrational enough to demonstrate any deterioration of his mental faculties.

By 1530, however, the year in which Henry turned 39, the ugly future was becoming manifest. The majority of Henry's newfound ill-will was expressed domestically, with increasing cruelties toward his wife and a more brazen courtship of Anne Boleyn. At this stage he still restrained his ire when dealing with public matters. When Thomas Abell, a loyal supporter of Katherina of Aragon, wrote a book in 1530 defending the legitimacy of her marriage to Henry, he incurred the king's "severe displeasure", but he wasn't executed.[51] However, the king's rationality and temper deteriorated until he had Abell imprisoned without warning in 1534 for having written the book four years earlier. It wasn't until 1540, ten years after Abell's rebellion, that he had Abell burned at the stake. It was

---

50   Lindsey, page 71.
51   It was also likely Henry could afford to be sanguine because he was still expecting a papal nullification of his first marriage. After all, papal annulments were reasonably common for nobility and royalty. Henry's best friend, Charles Brandon, had two marriages annulled before he married Henry's sister. Moreover, the children of annulled marriage could still be granted legitimacy by the pope. It was the support of Katherina's nephew, Charles V, which prevented Clement VII from granting the nullity suit. (Fraser, 1992 page 134-136).

completely irrelevant by that time. Both Anne and Katherina had been dead for years, and Abell's book was therefore no longer any threat to Henry's marriage plans. The priest's murder made sense to no one but Henry.

Henry's abrupt shift in behaviour is highlighted when it is examined over the course of his relationship with Anne Boleyn. Henry fell in love with her when he was 35 and executed her just before he turned 45. During the beginning of his relationship with Anne, he was a young man still lauded for his acumen and his chivalry, yet by the time he executed her in 1536 he was feared and reviled as a tyrant both domestically and abroad. At the beginning of their relationship, Henry adored Anne and they shared many intellectual pursuits and musical interests. For several years that's probably all they shared, since there is no evidence they ever consummated their relationship prior to their first secret wedding in November 1532. Some historians believe she rejected him because she did not love him or desire him, while others believe she did not love him but withheld her sexual favours as a strategy to become queen. Almost no one suggests that Anne refused to have sex with him because she had legitimate moral convictions against premarital intercourse, in spite of the lavish evidence of her piety. If it was wholly Anne's decision to refrain from sex for the roughly seven years of their courtship, it evinces that Henry wasn't a man to consider raping a woman by force, coercion or intimidation. He may now be considered a kind of minotaur, a beast that devoured women and men alike in its rage, but the younger Henry was nothing if not a gentleman.

Further indications of the change Henry was undergoing are demonstrated by his treatment of his long-suffering wife Katherina during the height of his passion for Anne. While he was still in his late 30s, the king always showed a modicum of kindness and gentility

Figure 6 - A vintage engraving showing
Anne Boleyn

toward the queen by maintaining Katherina's place at court.[52] He may have moved Katherina out of his adjoining rooms so he could install Anne in her place, but at least in public he showed Katherina respect and consideration. Although Katherina had been replaced in his affections and he was attempting to nullify their marriage, he publicly "praised her good qualities at length"[53]. Even when he was so smitten with Anne that he was mocked throughout Europe, he was still endeavouring to treat Katherina as decently as possible given the situation. That changed drastically after 1531. Except for some rare sporadic moments of benignancy, the king became vicious in his treatment of his first wife. He tortured her with petty emotional cruelties, such as demanding she turn over her jewels and her christening clothes to his new wife, as punishment for opposing his will. Repulsively, he celebrated when his former queen finally died in January 1536. This seems especially vile considering that with her last breath Katherina declared her unceasing love for the handsome prince she had married.

When Katherina died, Anne was pregnant and, despite Henry's occasional infidelities, was still reasonably secure in his affections. Yet within a few months the king had charged her with adultery and treason, charges that are almost unanimously considered fraudulent, and he had her beheaded on 19 May 1536. Henry seems to have convinced himself that, despite the ludicrousness of it, Anne had betrayed him with more than 100 men and was planning on poisoning his elder children[54]. The king's growing

---

52   Henry was occasionally out of sorts with his wife before 1531 , but any coolness between them never lasted long. In one instance he was angry with the queen because her father had betrayed his alliance with Henry. Another notable time he was upset with Katherina was when she had the audacity to be angry about the elevation of Henry's illegitimate son, Henry Fitzroy, to the title of the Duke of Richmond. She felt this was an insult to her and a threat to Mary's succession. Henry, who was more like a spoilt child than an adult at times, was irked with Katherina for not automatically approving of his actions.

53   Erickson, page 225.

54   Lindsey, page 128.

paranoia would send many other loyal courtiers to their deaths in the coming years.

After Anne's murder, the king's behaviour became nearly unrecognizable from that of the man he once was. He had become mentally unstable enough to set in motion plans to try Mary, his own daughter, for treason because she refused to agree with his claims about her mother and his right to be supreme head of the church. Relentless browbeating and a possible threat to her life finally intimidated Mary enough to give in. She submitted to her father's demands, signing a document declaring herself to be the illegitimate product of incest and repudiating one of the central tenets of her Catholic faith. Once Mary had capitulated to his blackmail, the king welcomed her back to court. When Mary was restored to him, Henry was quick to blame Anne Boleyn for the persecution his daughter had suffered, regardless of the fact that Anne had been dead for weeks by this time[55].

Henry's illegitimate son Henry Fitzroy died shortly after Anne Boleyn did. The king's behaviour upon learning of Fitzroy's death was bizarre to say the least. Henry ordered the Duke of Norfolk to bury Fitzroy in secret, perhaps because he feared the kingdom discovering he had no male heir at all. Norfolk followed Henry's directions, but when the king heard about the small funeral and the lack of mourners, he flew into a rage and threatened to imprison the duke in the Tower, much to the dumbfounded Norfolk's fear and consternation[56]. Obeying Henry had become as dangerous as disagreeing with him.

As he entered his mid-40s Henry became evermore capricious and prone to deadly rages. Henry's chief minister, Thomas Cromwell, became nearly "exasperated to the point of collapse by his master's childish irrationality [...] it became more and more clear that [Henry's] inner compass had gone awry"[57]. The courtiers and

55   Lindsey
56   Erickson
57   Erickson, page 254.

diplomats who saw him daily became increasingly afraid because no one could be certain what the king would do next. No one was safe. Henry would now turn suddenly against long-time friends and relations and have them killed on the slightest pretext. Even Jane Seymour was not safe from the king's anger. When his latest queen begged him to restore the monasteries he had destroyed, he raged at her, "ordering her not to meddle in affairs of state and ominously reminding her of what happened to the last queen who had so meddled"[58].

Henry's condition continued to worsen. In 1538 Henry told one of the most notoriously lecherous men in his court to dance with Princess Mary and bait her with innuendos to ascertain whether or not she was indeed as innocent as she was rumoured to be[59]. Mary passed the test, but it was a sign of Henry's increasing instability that the once chivalrous king would devise this sort of experiment for his daughter.

In that same year, Henry confiscated the treasures of the shrine of St Thomas Becket at Canterbury and ordered the destruction of the shrine itself, to the horror of his subjects. The king was now so erratic in matters of religion that he had people burned at the stake for daring to dispute the Catholic doctrine of transubstantiation even as he destroyed Catholic property[60]. Since the king found displeasure with elements of both Catholicism and Protestantism, there was almost no one of any faith who could be safe from religious persecution at his whim. This is such a radical departure from the learned theologian Henry had been formerly that it almost demands a pathological explanation in order to be understandable.

As he aged, Henry was increasingly paranoid and it is "hardly surprising that his paranoia took the form of a many-pronged attack on his cousins of royal blood living in England"[61]. He executed

---

58   Lindsey, page 131.
59   Erickson
60   Erickson
61   Fraser, page 294.

his cousins Henry Pole, Lord Montague and Henry Courtenay, 1st Marquess of Exeter in 1539, mainly for the crime of being too closely related to him and thus potential claimants to the throne. He also imprisoned their sons. The Marquess of Exeter's son, Edward Courtenay, was only 12 years old at the time of his arrest, and was imprisoned for *fifteen years* before being released by Mary I during the first few weeks of her reign. Lord Montague's son was not as lucky. He died in the Tower at an unrecorded date.

Displays of Henry's advancing cognitive decline continued to accumulate. In 1540 the king needed to marry for political reasons. He ordered a portrait of Anna of Cleves brought to him, and once he decided she was suitably attractive for a middle-aged, obese king with constantly seeping sores on his leg, Henry negotiated their betrothal. The king also decided he was in love with his unmet fiancée. He was so adamant about his love that he abruptly chose to surprise his bride-to-be by riding ahead to Rochester Abbey, where she was lodged, and burst into her rooms dressed as a messenger in order to dazzle her with his ardour. Once he met Anna of Cleves, however, he decided she was a "Great Flanders Mare" and he wanted to get out of the marriage.[62] [63] He also insisted that simply by feeling her breasts and belly on their wedding night he could tell Anna of Cleves was not a virgin. However, her virginity was miraculously restored when Henry needed it to provide a way out of the marriage. After a short while their union was annulled and Anna, who was given manor houses and a rich annuity, remained

---

62   Lindsey, page 136.

63   Henry's conviction that he was forced to marry an ugly woman against his will by cruel members of his court had little, if any, validity. In spite of Henry's slander, Anna of Cleves was not ugly. Her portrait clearly shows her to be a reasonably attractive woman. The royal portrait artist who painted her, Hans Holbein, was renowned for the accuracy of his portraits. Henry retained Holbein's services after meeting Anne, so he must have rendered her accurately enough to escape the king's wrath, which was no mean feat at this time. Moreover, Henry did not dismiss, imprison or behead anyone who had actually seen her beforehand and had reported to him that she was very pretty

in England as the king's "cherished sister"[64]. He then summarily executed Thomas Cromwell for having successfully arranged the match when Henry told him to. Although his behaviour towards Anna of Cleves could be seen as merely self-centred and petulant, the reasons he gave for wanting the annulment and his retaliation against Cromwell are so irrational as to beggar understanding.

Henry marked Cromwell's execution by marrying his fifth wife, Katheryn Howard, the same day. No one was very surprised that Henry remarried so soon after he annulled his marriage to Anna of Cleves. His reputation for emotional vagary had become legendary, and Martin Luther scathingly declared that, "Junker Heinz will be God and does what he lust"[65]. Katheryn had a kind, very compliant personality, inspiring Henry to choose as her motto "no other wish save his"[66]. Henry found her easy-going temper endearing and lauded her as his "rose without a thorn"[67]. When the king discovered that his new wife would rather flirt with a handsome young man named Thomas Culpepper[68] instead of being required to fondle the "old, pus-oozing flesh beneath the king's robes"[69], the king was distraught and enraged. He sobbed, complaining that he had been burdened with "such ill-conditioned wives" and insisted his council members were at fault "for this last

---

64   Lindsey, page 157.
65   Lindsey, page 152.
66   Lindsey, page 165.
67   Erickson, page 313.
68   This was probably the same Thomas Culpepper who was an accused rapist and murderer. He raped a park-keeper's wife in front of several witnesses and when a bystander tried to intervene to help the woman being assaulted, Culpepper killed him. Culpepper was, rather ironically, pardoned for his crimes by Henry VIII, mainly because the victims were from a low social caste (Lindsey, 1995, page 168). I am unable to suppress my lack of professional detachment and must admit that I find it delightful that he was publicly executed. I sincerely hope that the woman that he had raped, and the family of his murder victim, were all in the watching crowd to enjoy his beheading.
69   Lindsey, page 164.

mischief"[70], because they had urged him to wed Katheryn. Henry was clearly becoming wildly detached from reality.

The king was growing ever more inclined to murderous fickleness. In 1541 he executed the 68-year-old Countess of Salisbury, Margaret Pole, because she had the audacity to have given birth to children who were too closely related to him, and were therefore too close to his throne. It didn't matter that her threat to Henry was non-existent. In his paranoid state the king saw the elderly countess as a source of danger. So sudden was his decision to dispatch her that there was no time to send for an experienced executioner. The hapless axeman failed to behead the countess in the first stroke, and hacked at her neck and shoulders repeatedly until he had finally mutilated her enough to kill her. Henry VIII, the same man that Erasmus wrote of as having "revived the virtues of the ancient heroes" and who "appeared to incarnate all the ardent vitality of Christian Knighthood", had become a monster who slaughtered frail widows[71]. This is a personality change so extreme that it is hard to see it as *not* rooted in a mental illness of some kind.

Henry's paranoia put everyone around him at risk. One of the French ambassadors to the English court warned that Henry suffered from the "plague" of "distrust and fear. This King, knowing how many changes he has made, and what tragedies and scandals he has created, would fain keep in favour with everybody, but does not trust a single man, expecting to see them all offended, and he will not cease to dip his hand in blood as long as he doubts his people. Hence every day edicts are published so sanguinary that with a thousand guards one would scarce be safe. Hence too it is that now with us, as affairs incline, he makes alliances which last as long as it makes for him to keep them"[72]. Everyone was aware that Henry had become as irrational and suspicious as he was dangerous. Lord Montague, a member of Henry's court, warned

---

70   Smith
71   Erickson, page 74.
72   CPS Vol.15, pages 481-488.

his fellow courtiers that the king would "be out of his wits one day
[…] for when he came into his chamber he would look angrily, and
after fall to fighting"[73].

Henry's increasing ill health did not deter him from marrying
again after he beheaded his fifth wife in February of 1542. He
wedded Catherine Parr, the widowed Lady Latimer, in 1543, not
long after his 52nd birthday. He had become such a tyrannical
butcher that his subjects were almost blasé about his behaviour. An
Englishman named Richard Hilles wrote to a friend in September
that "our King has within these 2 months … burnt 3 godly men in
one day. For in July he married the widow of a nobleman named
Latimer; and he is always wont to celebrate his nuptials by some
wickedness of this kind"[74]. It is a credit to the wisdom and acting
abilities of his final wife that she only came close to losing her head
once, when Henry became angry with her because she had corrected
him on a point of theology. Religion was extremely important to
Catherine, which may explain why she lapsed in her safe deference
to Henry's opinions. Henry issued a warrant for her arrest, which
was quickly relayed to her via her allies at court. She had hysterics,
either a real fit because she feared – not unreasonably -- for her
life, or histrionics designed to convince Henry of her deferential
opinions. Henry's physician, a friend and religious sympathizer of
the queen, told the King that his majesty's displeasure had made
Catherine "dangerously ill"[75]. Henry was placated and Catherine
was spared. In one of the major mood swings that Henry frequently
experienced, when his uninformed chancellor attempted to arrest
the queen the next day, the king attacked him and berated him for
his audacity.

Henry was also behaving erratically in the larger world of
European politics. In the middle of 1544 Henry went off to fight
yet another pointless war with France, leaving his queen as regent to

73   Erickson, page 288.
74   CSP Vol.18(2) pages 26-30.
75   Lindsey, page 198.

deal with the intermittent war between England and Scotland. The Scots, having no real desire to join their kingdom with England or subjugate themselves to the English king, had backed out of an agreement to have the infant Mary Queen of Scots wed Henry's young son prince Edward. Incensed by the thought that they were rejecting his son and thwarting his attempts to unite Scotland and England under one crown, Henry sent Edward Seymour to launch an attack on the impudent Scots, regardless of the fact it was a war he could ill afford. The resulting five years of war was termed the "Rough Wooing" and strengthened anti-English feeling in that country so much that he lost any chance he may have had to bind the two kingdoms with marriage[76].

Henry's unchecked impulses and temper meant that England was fighting a war on two fronts. Since the king has squandered his wealth on foolishness for too long, both campaigns were strained from a lack of resources. Nonetheless, poor planning and poor leadership would have turned Henry's war in France into a disaster even if he had been flush with funds[77]. Henry's one success came on 14 September 1544, when his forces captured Boulogne, a city in northern France. Boulogne was less than 100 miles from London and could have potentially been used as a stronghold for future English invasions, but further penetration into French soil had become impossible because Henry had run out of the money needed to wage war[78]. The king couldn't afford to fund his own armies or hire more mercenaries to fight for him. Europe was aware that the English Lion was becoming toothless, and the idea of military retaliation from England was more sneered at than otherwise. When Henry became furious that England's ally, Charles V, decided to start negotiating a peace with France without

---

76   Magnússon, page 323.
77   Scarisbrick, pages 448-451.
78   Pollard, page 412.

Figure 7 - Henry lies in his death bed in
"Edward VI and the Pope: An Allegory of the Reformation",
artist unknown.

any English input, the emperor was completely indifferent to the King of England's meltdown over the accord[79].

By the summer of 1545, England was dealing with a plethora of difficulties as a result of the king's ineptitude. Worst of all, England was in serious danger of being invaded simultaneously by two foreign powers from multiple fronts[80]. This threat existed mainly because of Henry's ill-thought-out attacks on France and Scotland, which had only helped cement the Franco-Scots alliance against England and created an opportunity and reason for retaliation against his kingdom. His antagonistic dismissal of the dangers the Franco-Scots alliance presented is just one of many black marks on Henry's record as king.

Henry's savagery lasted until the very end of his life. In December 1546, just a few weeks before his death, the king turned his spite toward the Howard family. First, Henry had the Duke of Norfolk thrown into the Tower, stripping him of his titles and lands. Then, with malice aforethought, the king had the duke's son, the famous soldier and poet Henry Howard, the Earl of Surrey, charged with high treason based on piffles[81]. There was no real reason for Henry to have turned on the Howards in that manner. Norfolk was hated by many people and was indisputably a wretched human being but he had always fawned before Henry and subjugated himself to the king's commands[82]. Why did the king turn so suddenly and so violently against Norfolk and Surrey?

The likeliest reason is because the Earl of Surrey carried a threat to Henry's dynasty in his veins. Surrey's maternal grandfather, Edward Stafford, 3rd Duke of Buckingham, was a direct male descendant of King Edward III, and technically Surrey had a

---

79   Scarisbrick, pages 450-451.
80   Scarisbrick, pages 454.
81   Smith, 1970, pages 289-296.
82   Scarisbrick, 1970 page 484.

more legitimate right to wear the English crown than did Henry himself[83].

Notwithstanding Henry's penchant for beheading cousins, it must be said that the king may not have been the true culprit in Surrey's murder. The Seymour family, who were well-placed to reap the benefits of a nephew as king, hated the Howards. Surrey in particular considered the Seymours to be jumped-up rabble more fit for the king's sculleries than the king's council, and he was not hesitant to share this opinion. The evidence that the Seymours, rather than Henry, killed Surrey is persuasive[84].

The Earl of Surrey's coat of arms was the method used to arrange his execution. Chancellor Wriothesley, a man who had tortured Reformers and conspired to arrest Catherine Parr, was able to procure testimony from a herald by the name of Christopher Barker stating that Surrey had knowingly and rebelliously used the insignia of the English king Saint Edward the Confessor on his coat of arms[85]. Bearing the arms of Edward the Confessor without royal permission could easily be construed as treason, since it flaunted a connection to the throne equal to the king's[86]. Nonetheless, there is good historical evidence that Surrey was never told he was forbidden to bear Edward the Confessor's designs in his arms[87]. Disregarding the lack of evidence as always, Surrey was executed on 19 January 1547. Unlike many of the king's other victims, the earl did not follow the social conventions for those who were condemned. He did not go quietly or request that people pray for their sovereign. Instead, Surrey took the opportunity to castigate Henry from the scaffold, bellowing out, "Of what have you found me guilty? Surely you will find no law that justifies you; but I know that the king

---

83   Childs, page 24.
84   Sessions
85   Sessions, pages 396-398.
86   Smith, 1970, pages 290-291.
87   Sessions, pages 398-397.

wants to get rid of the noble blood around him, and to employ none but low people"[88].

Henry Howard was only 30 years old when he died, and in the prime of his creativity. The epitome of a Renaissance man, Surrey was renowned both as a warrior and one of the innovative forces behind the English sonnet form of poetry. Among modern literary scholars, he is remembered for his "extraordinary invention and influence" and his "position as the center of an English poetic tradition"[89]. For his contemporaries the Earl of Surrey was a luminary, gifted with both the pen and the sword. His execution was lamented throughout Europe and seen as further evidence of the king's despotic nature. Surrey's death would probably be much more historically denounced if it didn't seem to be just one more bloody travesty at the end of a long list of nightmarish miscarriages of justice perpetrated during Henry's reign.

Henry died on 28 January 1547. He was in denial about his own mortality, even at the very end. He was asked if he wished for a priest to come to him but he characteristically put it off because it was an unpleasant thought, saying he would "take a little sleep" first[90]. It was as if he hoped he could ward off death by avoiding his last confession, or perhaps he felt he could avoid death by refusing to think about it. Death nonetheless came for him in spite of everything Henry did to avoid it. After a lifetime of bold action and ripping the kingdom asunder with his needs, the king simply slipped from sleep into a coma and never awoke[91].

---

88   Sessions, page 409.
89   Dimmock, page 117.
90   Smith, 1982, page 313.
91   Smith, 1982, page 313.

Theories regarding Henry's mental aberrations

One of the theories to address Henry's increasingly paranoid and irrational behaviour after midlife is the hypothesis that the king had myxoedema. This illness is a by-product of hypothyroidism, a medical condition in which the thyroid gland doesn't make enough of the hormones it is supposed to produce[92]. Myxoedema could certainly have caused some of Henry's physical problems – including the weight gain, constipation, muscle pains and erectile dysfunction – that beset him after his middle-age. The presence of this illness could also explain some of his psychological ailments, such as his chronic depression, mental abstractions, irritability and mood instability. Nonetheless, there are two main weaknesses in this hypothesis. The first is the minor problem that Henry did not appear to show other signs typical of myxoedema, such as brittle nails, intolerance of the cold, slurred speech, or a goitre. The more significant problem is also that myxoedema is much more common in women over 50 than it is in men. Although this does not mean a younger man could *not* have this condition, it does lower the *likelihood* that he had it.

In 2005, historian Robert Hutchinson offered the idea that Cushing's syndrome, a disease involving the endocrine system, was the possible cause of Henry VIII's mental and emotional deterioration[93]. Henry indisputably displayed some of the symptoms of Cushing's syndrome, including rapid weight gain, particularly in the torso and face, muscle weakness of the hips, slower healing of wounds or abrasions, fatigue, headaches and impotence. It could have also caused some of his psychological disturbances, including depression, paranoia and anxiety. Additionally, he may have experienced the growth of a "buffalo hump" and a "moon face", where fat pads along the collarbone and on the back of the neck swell to unnatural proportions. Hutchinson also argues that Cushing's syndrome could explain the ulcers on Henry's legs. Cushing's can cause hypercalcemia, an elevated level of calcium in the blood that can lead to the death of the skin tissue, also known as skin necrosis. Hypercalcemia is a rare complication of Cushing's, but it is certainly possible. Notwithstanding the credibility of the theory, it does have a crucial weakness. The major problem with the hypothesis is that Cushing's syndrome cannot explain why the king's personality altered *before* he began to put on so much additional weight. Additionally, there is no evidence that Henry had a buffalo hump, or that his moon face was anything more than the normal jowly appearance of an obese older man. A diagnosis of Cushing's syndrome fits many of Henry's symptoms but it cannot completely solve the puzzle of the king's health.

The theory that Henry had land-bound scurvy because the foods he usually ate lacked, or were extremely low in, vitamin C was suggested by Susan Maclean Kybett in 1989. She argues that

---

93   Hutchinson

low levels of vitamin C in Henry's diet during parts of the year would account for his mood swings and physical deterioration[94]. There are several significant problems with the scurvy hypothesis, however, including the fact that for the wealthy there was a year-round availability of foods rich in vitamin C. Doctors of the era also recommended eating citrus fruits for those who could afford them. This was to maintain one's humoral balance[95]. It was also considered medically sound for a meal to end with a dessert containing pears, which were readily available in Tudor England and are a decent source of vitamin C as well. Even people in the lower income strata consumed a fair amount of foods containing vitamin C from locally grown produce that was dried, preserved in syrups, or pickled for consumption during the winter months. While Henry would have been unlikely to eat cabbage, which has abundant vitamin C, even very wealthy Tudors were fond of desserts made of vitamin C rich gooseberries. Better yet, the upper classes frequently put dried currants in meat dishes and desserts. Popular cakes and savoury pies containing currants and/or raisins were eaten at Christmas and during Lent, indicating that dried currants were customarily used in foods even during the winter months. A single cup of black European currants contains 338% of the recommended daily amount of vitamin C, which would have allowed Henry to avoid scurvy. Finally, Henry's doctors stuffed the king with as much rhubarb as he would eat. Rhubarb, which was thought to combat Henry's melancholy, is abundant in vitamin K and a reasonable source of vitamin C as well. It is very unlikely that Henry had scurvy.

Syphilis is also given as an explanation for Henry's psychological variations, as well as for the reproductive troubles his wives suffered. The initial symptoms of paralytic dementia in tertiary syphilis, such as socially inappropriate behaviour, increasing

94   Kybett
95   Adamson, page 227.

impairment of cognition and mood swings, appear to markedly align with Henry's irrational actions and thought processes later in life. However, the deterioration of mental faculties from syphilis would have presented differently than the canny madness Henry VIII displayed. Brain impairment caused by late stage syphilis is called general paralysis of the insane or paralytic dementia, and while it does have the sudden onset and change in personality like Henry experienced, it is much less able to be mistaken for "normal" behaviour. Rather than setting cunning traps for members of his court, he would have become clinically insane and clinically imbecilic. He would have been unmistakably what they would have perceived as a "madman", and he would have probably been unable to hold onto power. Theorists will have to look elsewhere for the cause of Henry's emotional and mental instability.

Although Henry's mental imbalance had become extreme by the end of his reign, few historians have actually called Henry VIII a lunatic. Instead, he has been described as "villainously quixotic"[96] or as "an imperious and dangerous autocrat who [was] mesmerized by his own legend"[97]. The descriptors of Henry's inconstancies have always left the impression that he was somehow in charge of his own fickleness, and that there was more method than madness in his actions. Some historians postulate that Henry began his "significant shift in personality" because he was "taking on the lineaments of mature kingship"[98], with others maintaining that Henry's eventual tyranny can be best explained by the fact he grew older and more aware of his power[99]. Alternatively, scholars argue that it was a change in circumstances and threats to his rule that pushed him into becoming a more ruthless monarch, possibly exacerbated by a blow to the head[100]. Some assert that the monster had always been

---

96   Erickson, page 267.
97   Weir, 2001, page 349.
98   Erickson, page 253.
99   Scarisbrick, 1970; Smith, 1982.
100   Lipscomb

present, but before his attempt to end his marriage to Katherina of Aragon, no one had ever really challenged his will on anything important, and thus his true malevolence had lain dormant[101]. In spite of the differing theories, there is a general consensus that his moodiness, paranoia and erratic behaviour became more extreme, and therefore more noticeable, in his later middle age.

One of the explanations of Henry's behaviour not involving mental illness but acknowledging the king's behaviour may have had medical roots is the idea that the king sustained a brain injury. Some historians suggest that one notable jousting accident in January 1536 may have led to an alteration in his personality[102], and the public has become largely aware of that theory, but fewer people know or remember that in the early 1950s an English physician argued that it was Henry's head injury in 1524 that is the true culprit behind the king's alteration[103].

Taking the postulations in reverse order, did the accident in 1536 hurt Henry's brain so severely that he became almost a different person? During one of the tournaments he held to celebrate his first wife's death, Henry was unhorsed and knocked senseless, remaining unconscious for more than two hours[104]. Some people have theorized that the king sustained brain damage in this jousting accident, and it was the resulting intracranial haemorrhage that caused him to change so drastically. It is possible that the strong blow to the head during the accident could have caused a blood clot in his brain, which in turn would have created intracranial pressure and pushed his brain forward in his skull, squashing the frontal lobe against the inside of his forehead. The frontal lobe of the brain is considered to be the centre of an individual's personality. Although an injury like this would not necessarily impair his motor functions, it could have caused serious

---

101   Lindsey
102   Lipscomb
103   McNalty
104   Lipscomb, page 58.

psychological problems. Some symptoms of a brain injury are lethargy, difficulty in concentrating, memory issues, bad judgment, depression, irrationally moody behaviour, emotional outbursts, insomnia, a low sex drive and radical personality changes[105]. The personality changes can be so severe that it is comparable to having schizophrenia.

Although such an injury could potentially be the cause of a personality change such as Henry's, as well as his mood swings and depression, it was unlikely to be the only source of the king's alteration. Henry was already exhibiting signs of mental change *before* his accident. He was definitely becoming irascible as early as 1532 and he started his first judicial killing spree in 1535. Before the age of 40, the king seldom executed someone he knew personally, having to be pushed to such extreme measures by his chancellors if there was a clear and present danger to his throne. An older Henry showed no such hesitation. In fact, he had begun to order the agonizing deaths of his subjects and courtiers for the flimsiest of reasons, or sometimes for no reason at all.

The first sign of Henry's new bloodthirstiness was the execution of three Carthusian priests and a Bridgettine monk on 4 May 1535, more than a year before the king would kill Anne Boleyn[106]. The monks had enraged Henry by their steadfast, treasonous, belief that the pope was the head of the church. Henry ordered the full traitors death for them, a nasty business involving being hung, then let down from the noose before they died from lack of oxygen, then being disembowelled and castrated while still conscious and having their entrails burnt in front of them. Once they were dead their bodies were cut into quarters and the heads chopped off. There is even a rumour that their castrated privates were stuffed into their mouths to stop their ceaseless prayers, but historians are not sure

---

105   Cifu and Caruso, page 52.
106   Starkey, page 523; Bernard, pages 167-168.

whether this is the truth or merely a rumour spread to strengthen Henry's reputation for barbarism.

On 19 June, he sent three more Carthusians to the same hideous death, including one named Sebastian Newdigate, a man who had once been one of Henry's courtiers before he renounced his earthly wealth and joined the religious order[107]. Newdigate appears to have been the first of the king's personal friends or acquaintances to be executed in connection with Henry's Great Matter. The king himself attempted to persuade Newdigate to change his mind about the pope's supremacy. According to the *Catholic Encyclopedia* of 1913, Newdigate "was thrown into the Marshalsea prison, where he was kept for fourteen days bound to a pillar, standing upright, with iron rings round his neck, hands, and feet. There he was visited by the King, who offered to load him with riches and honours if he would conform. He was then brought before the Council, and sent to the Tower, where Henry visited him again"[108]. Newdigate refused to acquiesce to Henry's wishes or accept the validity of Henry's arguments and died with his fellow Carthusians.

Although Henry's injury in 1536 could have made him decidedly worse, it couldn't explain why he had turned "bad" in the first place.

What about the head injury from 1524? If Henry had begun to show signs of growing instability in 1527, wouldn't that account for his behaviour by 1535? It is decidedly plausible, considering that head injuries can leave a person with "Jekyll and Hyde" - like dual personalities, or turn them outright into strangers full of anger and anxiety[109]. Henry would shift between his normative good-natured self into a monster of paranoid rage, and a traumatic brain damage could explain it. Nevertheless, there are some gaps in the theory. Most significantly is the fact that from 1527 to 1532 there are no signs of extreme personality changes in the king. Rumours had

107   Marshall,page 27.
108   The Catholic Encyclopedia, page 630
109   Cromer

swirled for years that he would put Katherina of Aragon aside in favour of a new, young and hopefully son-producing bride, so his decision to end his marriage was not a sudden one. Until the summer of 1532, Henry continued to treat Katherina with the same unstinting courtesy he had shown her during the halcyon days of their marriage. Although he was increasingly impatient and callous in his behavior toward his first wife and eldest daughter for the two years prior, it wasn't until after 1533 that the king became outright cruel to them in a seemingly short space of time, and only in his later years that he became uniformly tyrannical. Usually, brain impairment is less progressive than that. It manifests within a week or so after the injury and doesn't slowly go downhill over time. Instead, the undamaged sections of the brain learn to compensate for and assume the 'responsibilities' of the injured area, helping the patient get better – not worse – as the years pass. On average it takes between ten to fifteen years for people with severe brain injuries to show marked signs of improvement. If anything, ten to fifteen years after his jousting accident, 1534 -1539, Henry had only *begun* to behave like a brute.

Some historians and scholars have actually broached the topic of Henry's possible mental illness. Among these theories are that he was a psychopath, a sociopath, had narcissistic personality disorder, suffered from bipolar disorder, or was afflicted with clinical depression. Was Henry an autocratic ruler, a psychotic monster, or a man in the grip of unaccountable brain chemistry that undermined his decision making capabilities?

A significant flaw in any theory about Henry's mental condition is that psychological theories are based largely on "**weird**" people, i.e. the subject of psychology experiments are usually **W**estern, **E**ducated, from **I**ndustrialized and relatively **R**ich societies, which are usually in **D**emocratic countries. The king was more royal "we" than royal weird. He was Western and … that is about it. He was educated as much as possible for his era, but his education assured him that the planets affected his humours and that the sun revolved around the earth. England was not particularly industrialized, or comparatively rich, and beyond contestation it was not a democracy. Trying to measure Henry against a modern person may mean that psychologists are using a yardstick to try to measure cubic litres.

Professor Kevin Dutton, a psychologist and an affiliate member of Magdalen College at Oxford, used Robert D Hare's Psychopathy Checklist-Revised to assess Henry, and he found that the king was probably a psychopath. According to Dutton, the king had a score of 174, and anything over 168 put him firmly in psychopathic territory. Dutton was quoted as saying that Henry "scored very highly for emotional detachment and cold-hearted ruthlessness"[110]. When one looks at some of Henry's behaviour as an older king, such as the wanton destruction of cousins he had grown up with and with whom he had been good friends, it certainly seems that Dutton is justified in his opinion of Henry, but does this apply to the actions of the younger king? Psychopathology isn't something you can grow into or out of. You are either born a psychopath or you are not. Thus, Henry's emotional detachment and cold-hearted ruthlessness should have been consistent throughout his life, but it was not.

What would have been some of the other tell-tale signs that Henry was a psychopath? According to the *Encyclopedia of Mental Disorders*, the traits of psychopaths are a "glib and superficial charm, grandiose (exaggeratedly high) estimation of self, need for stimulation, pathological lying, cunning and manipulativeness, lack of remorse or guilt, shallow affect (superficial emotional responsiveness), callousness and lack of empathy, parasitic lifestyle, poor behavioural controls, sexual promiscuity, early behaviour problems, lack of realistic long-term goals, impulsivity, irresponsibility, failure to accept responsibility for own actions,

---

110   Yahoo News, 2013

many short-term marital relationships, [and] juvenile delinquency".
Which of these traits did Henry display, and if so – did Henry
show any of them prior to the 1530s?

Without question Henry was charming, but unlike most
psychopaths the king became less able to charm people as he grew
older. Psychopaths are so good at "gas-lighting", a form of emotional
abuse in which the abuser tries to convince the abused he or she
is at fault or in the wrong by denying abusive incidents occurred,
or altering the account of incidents so skilfully that the abused
becomes uncertain of reality and even convinced the abuser did
nothing untoward. They can keep supporters or make new ones,
even in egregious circumstances. Also, there is no evidence before
1530 that Henry's charm was superficial, rather than the genuine
charisma of someone who is not a psychopath.

Did Henry have a grandiose sense of self? How does one tell
with a king? Henry was raised in the conviction that royalty was
appointed by God Himself. He was taught that a monarch was the
epitome of the great chain of being and was therefore an *inherently
better* person than all other men. From birth he had been told that
the king and England are one and the same. With the exception
of believing himself to have become a god or messianic figure, it
would be hard for Henry to have grandiose ideas about his worth.
An argument for grandiosity is, of course, that Henry did declare
himself the supreme head of the Church of England, supplanting
the pope as religious authority. However, the king made that
decision based on a lot of encouragement from reformers and
lawyers like Thomas Cromwell, who persuasively argued that he
was the supreme head of the church and he should take up his
mantle. Henry did not try to declare himself pope and insist that
he had supplanted the Bishop of Rome in his ecclesiastical duties.

No one can deny that Henry had a need for stimulation, since
he constantly arranged entertainments such as hunting, dancing,
gaming and music for himself and his friends. This does not

necessarily fit into the psychopathic category, though. Extroverts also need stimulation and pleasant company, but that does not make extroverts axiomatically remorseless predators. There are too many other explanations for a man enjoying himself than psychopathology to account for it.

There is no sign that Henry was a pathological liar in his youth. In fact, the opposite was true. Psychopaths hate to lose any contest, regardless of how trivial, and will lie to win if at all possible. In contrast, in card games and other kinds of friendly gambling, the king didn't value winning enough to cheat or lie, because he frequently lost huge sums during games of cards or dice[111]. This means his courtiers also knew they could best him without fear of retaliation. This kind of enduring good sportsmanship is very unlikely if Henry were a psychopath.

It is true that as an older man the king was both cunning and manipulative. In 1543, the anti-reformist faction asked Henry for permission to arrest the reformist Archbishop of Canterbury, Thomas Cranmer, and imprison him in the Tower for heresy. When the king agreed to the scheme it seemed to be the end for Cranmer, but Henry sent for the archbishop and warned him of the plot, telling him that "false knaves will soon be procured to witness against you and condemn you"[112]. Henry then gave his royal ring to Cranmer, an act that carried extreme significance as it indicated the possessor was in the king's favour. When the anti-reformists sprang their ambush on Cranmer, he dramatically whipped out the ring he had been given, causing his enemies immediate and pronounced consternation. When the conservative coalition retreated to confer with Henry, they were "savagely rebuked" by the irate king[113]. Henry employed this kind of double-bind subterfuge to ensnare his courtiers multiple times during the final years of his reign[114].

---

111   Loades, page 96.
112   Scarisbrick, page 481.
113   Scarisbrick, page 481.
114   Smith, 1982, page 31.

HISTORY "In a Nutshell" SERIES

Yet these traps were noted because they were such a change from Henry's earlier style of kingship. Henry would waffle when he was younger, but it was because he was cautious, not cunning.

It is hard to see why anyone familiar with his marital history would think Henry had shallow emotional responses. He married his first wife when no one expected him to, because she was pretty and a damsel in distress, and he was publically devoted to her for almost twenty years. When he later wanted to divorce her and try for a male heir, he ripped holes in the fabric of European religion and politics to marry Anne Boleyn rather than make an "acceptable" marriage with a foreign noblewoman or princess. His love for Anne didn't turn into indifference -- it became scalding and implacable hate. He practically set up a shrine to Jane Seymour when she died shortly after the birth of their son. He could not keep a politically expedient marriage to Anna of Cleves functioning because he didn't *love* her enough. He wept and nearly had a breakdown when he found out his fifth wife, Katheryn Howard, had not been a virgin when they wed. He wanted to be married so much that he all but forced Catherine Parr to accept his proposal. Moreover, he retained a lifelong friendship with Charles Brandon, an emotional connection usually beyond the grasp of a psychopath. The king was not a man plagued by emotional detachment.

Did the king display a callous lack of empathy? A look at his behaviour after 1535 would make it impossible to argue otherwise. The older king was indubitably capable of slaughtering friends, family and spouses without any stronger feeling than feeling sorry for *himself.* Nevertheless, an older Henry is not the full story. When Henry was a freshly crowned monarch he eagerly tried to mend the rift the War of the Roses caused between the Tudors and his mother's family. In a reversal of his father's policy, the new king offered his Plantagenet kinfolk places at court, honoured them, and showed them royal favour[115]. Only one family member,

---

115   Starkey, page 306.

the Duke of Buckingham, was stupid enough to be anything but grateful. Buckingham didn't just want the king's friendship, he wanted the king's crown. The duke was so candid about his desire for the throne that it is somewhat mind-boggling. Buckingham bragged about prophecies which foretold that he would one day rule England, saying that God had killed the infant son born to Henry and Katherina of Aragon in order to punish the king and to pave the way for Buckingham's ascent. The duke also declared, openly, that the king would never have an heir. Buckingham's actions were brazenly treasonous. Henry, who had been incredibly patient in the matter, had no choice but to have his cousin executed in 1521, but he clearly did not enjoy the prospect[116]. His chancellor, Cardinal Wolsey, had to practically badger him into signing the death warrant. A young Henry was far from callous.

Insomuch as he was the king, it is impossible to determine whether or not Henry had a parasitic lifestyle. He was *expected* to live off taxes on the labours of others.

Then there is the question of whether or not Henry had poor behavioural controls or impulsivity. When he was an older man the king was certainly a slave to his impulses, but was this the case prior to the 1530s? His relationship with Anne Boleyn seems to indicate otherwise. Henry appears to have waited approximately seven years, from 1524/1525 until 1532, to consummate his union with Anne. It was only after years of frustration did he give up on the pope and wed Anne anyway. He never insisted that Anne give him her body as proof of her heart. He did not arrange to have his first wife murdered. He didn't promise to marry Anne and then jilt her for a more politically expedient and financially rewarding bride. He even dithered when it came to giving Cardinal Wolsey the chop, despite the fact the prelate had actually descended into treasonous activity in his hatred for Anne. Shortly before his death, Wolsey foolishly offered his clandestine support to Katherina in order to

---

116   Scarisbrick, 1970, pages 118-120.

frustrate Henry's plan to gain an annulment, and began "advising foreign powers on the best tactics to use against his sovereign" in an attempt to "foment unrest in England" and "coerce Henry into leaving Anne"[117]. When one compares Wolsey's slow fall from grace despite his guilt, and Cromwell's rapid fall from grace despite his innocence, it seems clear that Henry's behavioural controls had *become* poor rather than having always been poor.

Henry was also blessedly free from early behaviour problems or any signs of juvenile delinquency. In fact, he was positively cherubic as a child, and was possibly destined for the church. Not only was the infant Henry cute as a button, he was coddled by his mother in a way that was discouraged for his older brother, Arthur. His tutor, John Skelton, praised Henry not only for his keen mind, but for the boy's inherent commitment to the idea of chivalric virtues and pious attitude toward religion. Even when he was very young Henry was already showing the star quality and athleticism that made him so beloved in his early reign, and he seems to have been petted by everyone but his rather stern father.

Could Henry be accused of a lack of realistic long-term goals? Granted, he wanted to recover the former English territories on the continent, wresting them by force of arms from the French, but was that an unreasonable goal for a king? Was it ludicrous that he should want to "remake Camelot" in his own court, or just the sign of an idealist young man? For monarchs, there is a fine line between rational and irrational ambition, and Henry needs to be measured on that scale. What is known is Henry had no plans to become the next Alexander the Great and conquer the world, and he did not make elaborate plans to go on Crusade like Richard the Lionheart. A psychopath would have aimed higher, or have pretended to be content with lower.

Henry can be justly accused of irresponsibility as a youthful monarch, content to leave the governing of England to wizened

---

117   Starkey, page 428.

old men while he jousted, feasted, and impregnated his wife. This is not surprising in a young man who had led a sheltered almost cloistered existence prior to becoming king. Fun will always be more appealing than work. Furthermore, what is the difference between "irresponsible" and "good delegation" in a ruler? King John had been a micromanager and it had been a disservice to his country and his reign. Was Henry truly irresponsible to rely on older, more experience and learned counsellors? Nonetheless, Henry's decisions as an older king – such as to go hunting with Katheryn Howard rather than rule his country -- were certainly problematic. Yet self-indulgence is not always a sign of egomania or psychopathy and it is impossible to say for sure where Henry fit on this scale at any particular time in his life.

The supposition that Henry failed to accept responsibility for own actions relies entirely on how old Henry was at the time. Young Henry was not prone to blaming others for his mistakes, as demonstrated by a jousting accident in 1524 when he was inadvertently handed his lance and set on course before his visor was lowered. This error could have easily killed him. When his opponent's lance struck the king, it splintered and the potentially lethal shards blasted into Henry's face. Nonetheless, the king graciously forgave those responsible and insisted that "no one was to blame but himself"[118]. In contrast, an older Henry would blame Anne Boleyn for the beheading of Thomas More, and would blame her again – even though she was already cold in her grave – for his treatment of his daughter Mary. The aged king also irrationally blamed those around him for his marriage to Anna of Cleves, the judicial murder of Thomas Cromwell, and his choice of Katheryn Howard as a fifth bride. It is plain that Henry refused to accept responsibly after 1535, but not before it.

Finally, do Henry's many short-term marital relationships mark him as psychopath? Yes and no, because most were neither

---

118   Fraser, page 107.

short nor consummated nor left voluntarily. His initial marriage to Katherina of Aragon spanned more than two decades. His marriage to Anne was less than four years long, but the relationship itself lasted for more than ten years. His third marriage was short, but inasmuch as his wife died he can hardly be held accountable for its dissolution. His fourth marriage was one he was forced into and never consummated, so is not really the same thing as a wedding in Vegas that went south three months into it. The end of his fifth marriage was not wholly voluntary either, in that he hadn't fallen out of love with Katheryn, but instead had discovered what he believed to be treasonous behaviour. He remained married to Catherine Parr until his death, but in fairness it was a close shave for the queen. What is most curious about his marital record is that four out of five weddings occurred after his fortieth birthday. Was he psychopath after his birthday, but not before it?

One explanation for this may be that Henry was a sociopath. Whereas psychopaths are born, sociopaths are *made*:

> Researchers tend to believe that sociopathy is the result of environmental factors, such as a child or teen's upbringing in a very negative household that resulted in physical abuse, emotional abuse, or childhood trauma. Sociopaths, in general, tend to be more impulsive and erratic in their behaviour than their psychopath counterparts. While also having difficulties in forming attachments to others, some sociopaths may be able to form an attachment to a like-minded group or person. Unlike psychopaths, most sociopaths don't hold down long-term jobs or present much of a normal family life to the outside world. When a sociopath engages in criminal behaviour, they may do so in an impulsive and largely unplanned manner, with little regard for the risks or consequences of their actions. They may become agitated and angered

easily, sometimes resulting in violent outbursts. These kinds of behaviours increase a sociopath's chances of being apprehended.[119]

Did Henry become a sociopath? Part of the problem in answering that question is that phycologists are not exactly sure what makes a sociopath. In truth, it is as much as 50% genetics, and 50% "a confusing and not-yet-understood mixture of environmental factors"[120]. Childhood abuse has a strong correlation to sociopathology and we know that Henry did not have an abusive childhood, but not all sociopaths were abused as children so that cannot rule out the king. There may be physical factors as well. It appears to be possible to become a sociopath due to a traumatic brain injury[121], such as the one Henry sustained while jousting. Again, the problem with blaming Henry's behavioural change entirely on that incident is the timing. His behaviour had already become erratic and murderous several months – if not years -- before he entered the tilting field.

It is rare, if not unheard of, for a non-sociopathic adult to metamorphose into a sociopath. The roots of true sociopathology seem to lie in childhood. Notwithstanding that fact, affluence can lead people to occasionally *act* like sociopaths. Multiple psychological experiments have demonstrated that the sense of entitlement that comes with wealth and power makes people "more likely to cheat, lie and break the law than those who were poorer"[122]. Rich people are also exceedingly prone to lack empathy, caring little to nothing of the needs of others[123]. Although Marie Antoinette never said, "Let them eat cake!", this attitude is found in the affluent and influential more often than it is not. Additionally, moneyed individuals were more likely to "endorse essentialist lay

---

119   Grohol
120   Meyers
121   Stamatakis
122   Conley
123   Coleman

theories of social class categories (i.e., that social class is founded in genetically based, biological differences)" to explain why those who were less prosperous deserved to be so, and thus poverty did not pose a moral or social obligation on the wealthy for resolution[124]. This effect is entirely cultural. In psychological experiments where the wealthy could be induced to think of themselves as less wealthy, they were dramatically more compassionate[125]. A lack of empathy and compassion is the clearest, most distinctive trait of a sociopath, and it is obvious that wealth can induce people to mimic sociopathic behaviour. So, was Henry a sociopath, or was he just rich?

Other historians theorize that Henry was a narcissist who was prone to "brutality" and "deadly temper tantrums"[126], and that his condition was enhanced by a particularly severe crisis of generativity, more commonly known as a midlife crisis[127]. While the accusation of a midlife crisis is indisputable, the idea that Henry had narcissism is more open to debate. Everyone has a kernel of narcissism within them, but what most people think of as a narcissist is actually someone with Narcissistic Personality Disorder (NPD) – a person who has carried the normal infantile belief that the world revolves around them abnormally into adulthood. According to the *Diagnostic and Statistical Manual of Mental Disorders* (5th edition), to truly have NPD a person must have exaggerated self-appraisals and fluctuating self-esteem, goals that are influenced by a sense of entitlement, impaired empathy, superficial abilities to form relationships, as well as grandiose and attention-seeking behaviour. NPD usually display most of the following traits:

1. Has a grandiose sense of self-importance, e.g. exaggerates achievements and talents, expects to be recognized as superior without commensurate achievements.

2. Is preoccupied with fantasies of unlimited success, power,

---

124   Kraus and Keltner
125   The Economist, 2010
126   Lindsey, page 153.
127   Shore

brilliance, beauty or ideal love.

3. Believes that he or she is "special" and unique and can only be understood by, or should associate with, other special or high-status people, or institutions.

4. Requires excessive admiration.

5. Has a sense of entitlement, i.e. unreasonable expectations of especially favourable treatment or automatic compliance with his or her expectations.

6. Is interpersonally exploitative, i.e. takes advantage of others to achieve his or her own ends.

7. Lacks empathy: is unwilling to recognize or identify with the feelings and needs of others.

8. Is often envious of others or believes that others are envious of him or her.

9. Shows arrogant, haughty behaviour or attitudes.

Again, how do you evaluate these traits in a medieval monarch? Henry's self-importance was reality as much as any sense of grandiosity. It is true that Henry was preoccupied with ideal love and an ideal world of chivalry, but was it pathologically so? He did not have to merely believe himself to be special; he *was* special. Henry certainly loved to be the centre of attention, but his sense of entitlement was a legitimate one. He was actually entitled to being treated as … well, a *king*. Did he exploit others, or seek out relationships that would benefit him? Not really. Many a highborn nobleman bemoaned Henry's promotion of "low people", and he certainly didn't chose his brides because of the wealth and influence they could give him. Neither did Henry show excessive or unreasonable envy, and if he thought others were envious of him – that was based on observation, not narcissism. His arrogance cannot be assessed as narcissistic or not because it is impossible to find abnormal arrogance in a man who was believed by himself and others to be the best human being alive in his whole kingdom.

Henry had a huge ego, and liked to be fêted, but it is impossible to tell if he were a full-blown narcissist.

The NPD theory does have some definite points in its favour. It is bolstered by Henry's childhood. Like sociopaths, narcissism seems to be an acquired trait. It starts with a sensitive child who gets excessive praise or excessive criticism, leading the child to believe everything is all about him or her – either in a good way or a bad one. Children who are overindulged or told they have exceptional personal beauty may also develop NPD. Likewise, children who are overindulged by one parent and treated coldly by the other parent are at risk of become narcissistic. It is beyond doubt that Henry had a privileged, cosseted childhood and his beauty and intelligence could have done nothing but exacerbate his feelings of exceptionalism. Additionally, Henry was extremely close to his mother but appears to have had a chillier relationship with his more emotionally repressive father. Did Henry's lauded personal charms, combined with his mother's petting and his father's harsh criticism, shape the future king into a narcissist?

An argument against Henry having NPD, at least prior to the 1530s is the fact that the king did not go off the rails at the slightest hint of criticism. People with NPD have hugely inflated egos, but like a hot-air balloon their ego's huge size does not negate that it is fragile and lacks substance. Narcissists are terrified of any damage to the ego, because they fear that people will discover they are full of air and not much else. Thus, a narcissist dramatically overreacts to any kind of negative feedback, perceiving it as an attack where they are most vulnerable. Often they display "narcissistic rage" if they are questioned or criticized – blustering and projecting their own negative qualities onto others in order to deflect blame[128]. Narcissists cannot ever admit to having been in the wrong or having committed an error. A narcissist can no more tender a sincere apology that they can fly to the moon by flapping their

---

128   Seltzer

arms[129]. While this describes Henry's reactions from 1535 onward, it does not match Henry's behaviour as a younger man. Before that watershed year, people who criticized Henry did not wind up with their heads on a chopping block for their audacity.

For example, in 1532 a priest named William Peto preached an Easter sermon in which he asserted that Henry, who was in the congregation *listening*, would meet his end just like the Old Testament tyrant Ahab[130]. Peto warned the king that if he didn't mend his ways, then dogs would lick his blood from the stones just as they had licked Ahab's after his death in battle. Peto also strongly implied that Anne Boleyn was Jezebel reborn. Considering that Jezebel was conceptualized as the nadir of harlotry, an evil queen who had slaughtered prophets and replaced them with idol worshippers, this was a thundering theological condemnation of Anne. Henry was very angry, but he didn't go berserk or have Peto's head cut off. The king wisely looked for other solutions. First, he had one of the theologians who was on his side, a priest named Curwin, preach the following Sunday. Peto was away at the time, so it seemed like a choice opportunity to refute him. Things did not go according to Henry's plans, however, since another friar named Elstow stood up from among the assembled listeners and began loudly refuting Curwin[131]. Unsurprisingly, Peto and Elstow were called up in front of the king's council, where Henry and his chief ministers castigated the pair soundly. The friars stood their ground. When the Earl of Essex told them they should be stuffed into a sack and dropped into the Thames to drown, Elstow told Essex, "Threaten these things to rich and dainty folk who are clothed in purple, fare delicately, and have their chiefest hope in this world, for we esteem them not, but are joyful that for the discharge of our duties we are driven hence. With thanks to God we know the way to Heaven to be as ready by water as by land, and therefore we

---

129   Seltzer
130   Bernard, page 152.
131   Bernard, pages 152-153.

care not which way we go"[132]. Despite thumbing their noses at the king and disputing his assertions, these friars were freed and sent into exile[133]. They left England and settled in Antwerp, where Peto continued to needle Henry by publishing a book defending the legitimacy of Katherina's marriage to the king.

Beyond a doubt, Henry's behaviour in the last fifteen or so years of his reign can be described as a narcissistic, but up until that point the king had a swelled head, rather than NPD.

Insomuch as so many of Henry's theoretical diagnoses mention his depression, questioning whether or not the king was clinically depressed, seems superfluous. Yet what about the type of depression that was once labelled "manic depression" and is now called bipolar disorder? Were the king's radical personality changes due to the onset of this mental illness?

The National Institute of Mental Health explains that people suffering from "bipolar disorder experience unusually intense emotional states that occur in distinct periods called mood episodes. Each mood episode represents a drastic change from a person's usual mood and behaviour. An overly joyful or overexcited state is called a manic episode, and an extremely sad or hopeless state is called a depressive episode. Sometimes, a mood episode includes symptoms of both mania and depression. This is called a mixed state. People with bipolar disorder may also be explosive and irritable during a mood episode. Extreme changes in energy, activity, sleep and behaviour go along with these changes in mood."

Does this describe Henry? Like the other theories on Henry's mental health, it certainly fits the profile of the ageing king, but does not match the behaviour of the king when he was younger. When the king first ascended the throne, and for the next twenty-five years of his reign, records show that Henry was consistently active and sought out pleasurable pastimes daily. There is no evidence

---

132   Stone, page 277.
133   Bernard, page 153.

that he was experiencing mania, which is marked by notable and excessive elation, agitation, restlessness and risk-taking behaviour. Henry liked to go hunting every day, but he didn't try to jump over walls or have his hounds killed if the hunt failed. Nor did the king instigate drunken revels every night and indulge in orgies. He appears to have been cheerful, not hypomanic.

The biggest sign that Henry was not bipolar, at least until he was older than 40, is that to be bipolar, one must have "lows" as well as "highs". Henry's blue periods didn't begin to strike until the king was a much older man. Even during his early frustrations with his Great Matter, Henry was more irked than depressed about the whole mess. His courtiers and physicians would have noticed depressive episodes in the young king, which would have been thought to be the result of too much black bile leading to melancholy, just as they noticed the bleak periods Henry experienced in his late middle-age, so it is unlikely that it would have gone unmentioned if he had been despondent for very long. Any depressive episodes would have needed to have been lengthy and profound to qualify the king as bipolar, since there is no such thing as a short, mild depression stage in bipolar disorder.

Henry would, however, have depressive episodes later in life.

There has been one medical condition posited that would explain why Henry's emotional changes and physical deterioration began shortly before his 40th birthday and then rapidly accelerated until his death. If the supposition that Henry had a Kell positive blood type is correct, then he may have developed a disease which is exclusive to Kell positive individuals: McLeod syndrome. The illness resembles Huntington's disease and may operate in a similar fashion by causing the degeneration of the basal ganglia.[134] [135] Patients are typically healthy during their infancy and childhood[136], with the disease starting to put in an appearance around a person's 40th birthday and then growing progressively worse over time[137]. Although the majority of people with this illness don't normally begin to show mental/psychological symptoms until after midlife, "there is subclinical affectation of muscle and peripheral nerve already in the third decade"[138], which would explain why the king's athleticism was compromised after his mid-30s. McLeod syndrome would explain both the *specific* degeneration of Henry's leg muscles and his sudden and increasingly large behaviour changes in the 1530s.

There are many different kinds of psychopathology exhibited by patients with McLeod syndrome including, but not limited to, deterioration of memory and executive functions, paranoia, depression and socially inappropriate conduct[139].[140] This mental deterioration can become severe. In one notable case, a previously healthy man with a high degree of intelligence was hospitalized at the age of 39 with an initial schizophrenic episode[141], and it was determined that the patient's psychopathology was

---

134   Danek et al.
135   The basal ganglia are a group of nuclei in the brain called the caudate nucleus, putamen and globus pallidus. These nuclei are associated with the cerebral cortex, thalamus and brainstem. In humans the basal ganglia are believed to control a diverse group of functions, including motor control, cognition, learning and emotions.
136   Symmans et al.
137   Danek et al
138   Danek et al, page 762.
139   Danek et al.
140   Although it could be argued that the king had a cluster of mental and physical illnesses that merely mimicked McLeod's syndrome, such as a combination of narcissism and a degenerative nerve disease, Occam's razor would support the simplest diagnosis.
141   Three-quarters of persons with schizophrenia develop the disease between 16 and 25 years of age. Onset is uncommon after age 30, and rare after age 40.

actually a symptom of his worsening McLeod syndrome[142]. This demonstrates that "schizophrenia-like symptoms", which include personality changes, anxiety, paranoia, depression and a host of other psychopathological conditions, can be the "prominent initial clinical manifestation" of McLeod syndrome[143]. There is certainly substantial evidence to suggest that Henry underwent a significant personality change after his 40th birthday, in a manner consistent with the mental problems that are often linked to McLeod syndrome.

Henry would have received the genes to express McLeod syndrome from his mother's family, probably via Jacquetta of Luxemburg, just as he would have received the gene for the Kell antigen. McLeod syndrome is carried on the X-chromosome and is inherited from the patient's mother[144]. Few, if any, females express McLeod syndrome because of the Lyon effect.[145] [146] However, women are able to pass the gene on to their children, where it can be expressed in *some*, but not all, Kell positive male offspring[147]. The condition is rare enough that Henry's Kell-positive maternal uncles and great-uncle may not have ever manifested McLeod syndrome themselves.

---

142   Jung et al.
143   Jung et al, page 723.
144   Marsh
145   Symmans et al; Marsh
146   The Lyon effect is the inactivation of one of the X-chromosomes in female mammals. A geneticist named Mary Lyon postulated that if the Y-chromosome is tiny and the X-chromosome is very large, then females (XX phenotype) would have considerably more genetic material than males (XY phenotype) if both X-chromosomes were expressed. Thus, one of the two X-chromosomes in females is typically not expressed.
147   Wimer et al.

Conclusion

Considerable challenges face historians in their attempts to ascertain the truth. Piecing together the facts from the bits of information that survived for centuries is very difficult. Often information is gleaned from letters written about court gossip and that relay only second-hand knowledge. Additionally, the writers of those letters were not impartial. The court teemed with intrigue and factional jockeying for power. Those who were in the favour of certain ministers, or wives, of the king could view the same event very differently. It is even more difficult to make an accurate medical diagnosis using information gleaned from those same slanted historical records. While there are genetic markers for the suspected conditions and new techniques for extracting DNA from very old remains, so that if Henry's body were exhumed for analysis a DNA test could prove or disprove beyond doubt many of the medical theories about the king, the funds to dig Henry up are simply not available – even if the current queen would give researchers permission to do so. Until such analysis is allowed, historical clues will have to suffice in the search for answers regarding Henry's health and ambiguous reign.

Bibliography

Ackroyd, Peter. 2013. Tudors: The History of England from Henry VIII to Elizabeth I. Macmillan.

Adamson, Melitta Weiss. 2004. Food in Medieval Times. Greenwood Publishing Group.

Baichoo, V. and Bruce-Tagoe, A. 2000 "Recurrent hydrops fetalis due to Kell allo-immunization" Annals of Saudi Medicine Sep-Nov; 20(5-6):415-6.

Berkowitz RL, Beyth Y, Sadovsky E. "Death in utero due to Kell sensitization without excessive elevation of the delta OD450 value in amniotic fluid. Obstet Gynecol. 1982;60:746-749.

Bernard, G. W. 2005. The King's Reformation. Yale University Press.

Bowman, J.M., J.M. Pollock, F.A. Manning, C.R. Harman, and S. Menticogou. 1992. "Maternal Kell Blood Group Alloimmunization." Obstetricas and Gynecology 79: 239–44.

Berkowitz RL, Beyth Y, Sadovsky E. "Death in utero due to Kell sensitization without excessive elevation of the delta OD450 value in amniotic fluid. Obstet Gynecol. 1982;60:746–749.

Caine, M.E., and E. Mueller-Heubach. 1986. "Kell Sensitization in Pregnancy." American Journal of Obstertics and Gynecology January: 85–90.

Calandar of State Papers. 1862. Letters and Papers, Foreign and Domestic, of the Reign of Henry VIII.: Preserved in the Public Record Office, the British Museum and Elsewhere. Edited by John S. Brewer, Robert H. Brodie, and James Gairdner. His Majesty's Stationery Office.

Calandar of State papers. 1864. Letters and Papers, Foreign and Domestic, Henry VIII, Volume 2, 1515-1518. Edited by J. S. Brewer. Vol. 2. London: Her Majesty's Stationery Office. http://www.british-history.ac.uk/letters-papers-hen8/vol2/pp104-118.

Calandar of State Papers. 1875. Letters and Papers, Foreign and Domestic, Henry VIII, Volume 4, 1524-1530. Edited by J.S. Brewer. Vol. 4. London: Her Majesty's Stationery Office,.

————. 1896. Letters and Papers, Foreign and Domestic, Henry VIII, Volume 15, 1540. Edited by James Gairdner and R.H. Brodie. Vol. 15. London: Her Majesty's Stationery Office.

————. 1902. Letters and Papers, Foreign and Domestic, Henry VIII, Volume 18 Part 2, August-December 1543. Vol. 18. London: Her Majesty's Stationery Office.

————. 1920. Letters and Papers, Foreign and Domestic, Henry VIII, Volume 1, 1509-1514. Edited by J.S. Brewer. Vol. 1. London: Her Majesty's Stationery Office.

————. n.d. Letters and Papers, Foreign and Domestic, Henry VIII, Volume 16, 1540-1541.

————. n.d. Letters and Papers, Foreign and Domestic, Henry VIII, Volume 19 Part 1, January-July 1544.

Chalmers, CR, and EJ Chaloner. 2009. "500 Years Later: Henry VIII, Leg Ulcers and the Course of History." Journal of the Royal Society of Medicine 102 (12): 514–17. doi:10.1258/jrsm.2009.090286.

Chamberlin, Frederick. 1931. The Private Character of Henry the Eighth. Washburn.

Childs, Jessie. 2007. Henry VIII's Last Victim: The Life and Times of Henry Howard, Earl of Surrey. Macmillan.

Cifu, David X., and Deborah Caruso. 2010. Traumatic Brain Injury. Demos Medical Publishing.

Coleman, Daniel. 2015. "Rich People Just Care Less." New York Times. Accessed June 20. http://opinionator.blogs.nytimes.com/2013/10/05/rich-people-just-care-less/.

Conley, Mikaela. 2012. "Rich People More Likely to Be Unethical." ABC News, February 27. http://abcnews.go.com/blogs/health/2012/02/27/are-rich-people-unethical/.

Cressy, David. 1997. Birth, Marriage, and Death: Ritual, Religion, and the Life-Cycle in Tudor and Stuart England. Oxford University Press US.

Cromer, Janet M. 2012 "After Brain Injury: The Dark Side of Personality Change Part I" Psychology Today https://www.psychologytoday.com/blog/professor-cromer-learns-read/201203/after-brain-injury-the-dark-side-personality-change-part-i

F. Gary Cunningham, F. Gary., Norman F. Gant Kenneth J. Leveno, Larry C. Gilstrap, III, John Hauth, Katharine Wenstrom. 2001. Williams Obstetrics 21st ed. McGraw-Hill Professional

Danek, A., J.P. Rubio, L. Rampoldi, M. Ho, C. Dobson-Stone, F. Tison, W.A. Stmmans, et al. 2001. "McLeod Neuroacanthocytosis: Genotype and Phenotype." Annual Neurology 50: 755–64.

Dimmock, Matthew. 2006. "Henry Howard, Earl of Surrey." In The Oxford Encyclopedia of British Literature, edited by David Scott Kastan, 5:117–20. Oxford University Press.

Erickson, C. 1980. Great Harry. New York: St. Martin's Press.

Fraser, Antonia. 1992. The Six Wives Of Henry VIII. Orion.

Geifman-Holtzman,O., Wojtowycz M, Kosmas E, Artal R. 1997. "Female alloimmunization with antibodies known to cause hemolytic disease". Obstetrics and Gynecology, Feb;89(2):272-5.

Goh J T, Kretowicz E M, Weinstein S and Ramsden G H. 1993. "Anti-Kell in pregnancy and hydrops fetalis". Australian and New Zealand Journal of Obstetrics and Gynaecology, 33(2):210-211

Grohol, John M., and Psy D. ~ 3 min read. 2015. "Differences Between a Psychopath vs Sociopath." Psych Central.com. http://psychcentral.com/blog/archives/2015/02/12/differences-between-a-psychopath-vs-sociopath/.

Hu FB, Li TY, Colditz GA, Willett WC, and Manson JE. 2003. "TElevision Watching and Other Sedentary Behaviors in Relation to Risk of Obesity and Type 2 Diabetes Mellitus in Women." JAMA 289 (14): 1785–91. doi:10.1001/jama.289.14.1785.

Hu, Frank B. 2003. "Sedentary Lifestyle and Risk of Obesity and Type 2 Diabetes." Lipids 38 (2): 103–8.

Hutchinson, R. 2005. The Last Days of Henry VIII: Conspiracy, Treason and Heresy at the Court of the Dying Tyrant. London Phoneix: Weidenfeld &Nicolson 2005 Orion Books Ltd. 2006.

Ives, Eric William. 2004. The Life and Death of Anne Boleyn: "The Most Happy." Wiley-Blackwell.

Jung, H.H., and H. Haker. 2004. "Schizophrenia as a Manifestation of X-Linked McLeod-Nuerocanthocytosis Syndrome." Journal of Clinical Psychology 65: 722–23.

Katon, Wayne J., Carolyn Rutter, Greg Simon, Elizabeth H. B. Lin, Evette Ludman, Paul Ciechanowski, Leslie Kinder, Bessie Young, and Michael Von Korff. 2005. "The Association of Comorbid Depression With Mortality in Patients With Type 2 Diabetes." Diabetes Care 28 (11): 2668–72. doi:10.2337/diacare.28.11.2668.

Keynes M. The personality and health of King Henry VIII (1491–1547). J Med Biogr 2005;13:174–83

Kraus, Michael W., and Dacher Keltner. 2013. "Social Class Rank, Essentialism, and Punitive Judgment." Journal of Personality and Social Psychology 105 (2): 247–61. doi:10.1037/a0032895.

Kybett, S.M. 1989. "Henry VIII -- A Malnourished King?" History Today September: 19–25.

Lacey, Robert. 1972. The Life and Times of Henry VIII. Welcome Rain Publishers.

Larsen, CS. 1997. Bioarchaeology: Interpreting Behavior from the Human Skeleton, Cambridge University Press, Cambridge

Licence, Amy. 2014. The Six Wives and Many Mistresses of Henry VIII: The Women's Stories. Amberley Publishing Limited.

Lindsey, K. 1995. Divorced, Beheaded, Survived: A Feminist Reinterpretation of the Wives of Henry VIII. Reading, Massachusetts: Addison-Wesley Publishing Company.

Lipscomb, Suzannah. 2012. 1536: The Year That Changed Henry VIII. Lion Books.

Loades, D. M. 1992. Politics and Nation: England, 1450-1660. Headstart History Publishing

Luban

MacNalty, Arthure Salusbury. 1952. Henry VIII: A Difficult Patient. London: Christopher Johnson Publishers. http://www.royalcollection.org.uk/collection/1024816/henry-viii-a-difficult-patient.

Magnússon, Magnús. 2003. Scotland: The Story of a Nation. Grove Press.

Marshall, Peter. 2006. Religious Identities In Henry VIII's England. Ashgate Publishing, Ltd.

Marsh, W.L. 1990. "Biological Roles of Blood Group Antigens." The Yale Journal of Biology and Medicine 63: 455–60.

Marsh WL, Redman CM., 1987. "Recent developments in the Kell blood group system". Transfusion Med Rev. Apr;1(1):4–20.

Marsh WL, Redman CM. 1990. "The Kell blood group system: a review". Transfusion. Feb;30(2):158–167.

Marsh, W.L., E.F. Schnipper, C.L. Johnson, K.A. Mueller, and S.A. Schwartz. 1983. "An Individual with McLeod Syndrome and the Kell Bollod Group Antigen K(K1)." Transfusion 23: 336–38.

Matusiak, John. 2014. Wolsey: The Life of King Henry VIII's Cardinal. The History Press.

Mayne, K., P. Bowell, and G. Pratt. 1990. "The Significance of Anti-Kell Sensitization in Pregnancy." Clinical and Labratory Haematology 12: 379–85.

Meyers, Seth. 2013. "Understanding the Sociopath: Cause, Motivation, Relationship." Psychology Today. http://www.psychologytoday.com/blog/insight-is-2020/201304/understanding-the-sociopath-cause-motivation-relationship.

Murphy, C. 2001. "Second Opinions: History Winds Up in the Waiting Room." In The Atlantic, 287:16–18.

"Narcissistic Personality Disorder: MedlinePlus Medical Encyclopedia." 2015. Accessed June 20. http://www.nlm.nih.gov/medlineplus/ency/article/000934.htm.

Park, Bert E. 2015. Ailing, Aging, Addicted: Studies of Compromised Leadership. Lexington. The University of Kentucky Press.

Pollard, Albert Frederick. 1919. Henry VIII. Longmans.

Rao. 2008. Textbook of Gynaecology. Elsevier India.

"Rh Incompatibility: MedlinePlus Medical Encyclopedia." 2014. Accessed December 16. http://www.nlm.nih.gov/medlineplus/ency/article/001600.htm.

Robinson, Jon. 2013. Court Politics, Culture and Literature in Scotland and England, 1500-1540. Ashgate Publishing, Ltd.

Santiago, JC., Ramos-Corp, Oyonarte S, Montoya F. 2008. "Current clinical management of anti-Kell alloimmunization in pregnancy". European Journal of Obstetrics and Gynecology Reproductive Biology 136(2):151-154

Scarisbrick, J. J. 1968 (2003). Henry VIII. University of California Press.

Seltzer, Leon. 2011. "The Narcissist's Dilemma: They Can Dish It Out, But . . ." Psychology Today. http://www.psychologytoday.com/blog/evolution-the-self/201110/the-narcissists-dilemma-they-can-dish-it-out.

————. 2013. "6 Signs of Narcissism You May Not Know About." Psychology Today. http://www.psychologytoday.com/blog/evolution-the-self/201311/6-signs-narcissism-you-may-not-know-about.

Sessions, William A. 2003. Henry Howard, the Poet Earl of Surrey: A Life. Oxford University Press.

Shore, M.F. 1972. "Henry VIII and the Crisis of Generativity." Journal of Interdisiplinary History 2: 359–90.

Stamatakis, Jeannine. 2012. "Can You Make a Sociopath—Either Through Brain Injury or Other Types of Trauma?" Scientific Americna, August. http://www.scientificamerican.com/article/can-you-make-sociopath-through-brain-injury-trauma/.

Starkey, David. 2001. Elizabeth: The Struggle for the Throne. HarperCollins.

————. 2003. Six Wives : The Queens of Henry VIII. Chatto & Windus.

————. 2006. Monarchy: From the Middle Ages to Modernity. HarperCollins.

Stone, Jean Mary. 1904. Reformation and Renaissance (circa 1377-1610). Duckworth.

Stride, P., and K. Lopes Floro. 2013. "Henry VIII, McLeod Syndrome and Jacquetta's Curse." Journal of the Royal College of Physcians of Edinburgh 43 (4): 353–60.

Symmans, W.A., C.S. Shepherd, W.L. Marsh, R. Oyen, S.B. Shohet, and B.J. Linehan. 1979. "Hereditary Acanthocytosis Associated with the McLeod Phenotype of the Kell Blood Group System." Bristish Journal of Haematology 42: 575–83.

The Catholic Encyclopedia: An International Work of Reference on the Constitution, Doctrine, Discipline and History of the Catholic Church. 1913. The Encyclopedia press inc.

The Economist. 2010. "The Rich Are Different from You and Me," July 29. http://www.economist.com/node/16690659.

Tippett P., Lomas-Francis C, Wallace M. 1996 "The Rh antigen D: partial D antigens and associated low incidence antigens". Vox Sanguinis 70:123-131

Ward, Thomas. 1719. England's Reformation, (from the Time of K. Henry VIII. to the End of Oates's Plot.): A Poem in Four Cantos. E. More.

Warnicke, Retha M. 1991. The Rise and Fall of Anne Boleyn: Family Politics at the Court of Henry VIII. Cambridge University Press.

———. 2000. The Marrying of Anne of Cleves: Royal Protocol in Early Modern England. Cambridge University Press.

Weir, A. 2001. Henry VIII: The King and His Court. New York and Toronto: Ballantine Books.

Whitley, Catrina Banks, and Kyra Kramer. 2010. "A New Explanation for the Reproductive Woes and Midlife Decline of Henry VIII." The Historical Journal 53 (4): 827–48.

Wimer, B.M., W.L. Marsh, H.F. Taswell, and W.R. Galey. 1977. "Haenmatological Changes Associated with with the McLeod Phenotype of the Kell Blood Group System." British Journal of Haematology 36: 219–24.

Win, N. Kaye, T. Mir, N., Damain-Willems, C., Chatfield, C. 1996. "Autoimmune Haemolytic Anaemia in Infancy with Anti-Kpb Specificity" Vox Sanguinis 71 (3):187-188

Illustrations

About the Author

Kyra Cornelius Kramer is an author and researcher with undergraduate degrees in both biology and anthropology from the University of Kentucky, as well as a masters degree in medical anthropology from Southern Methodist University. Her work is published in several peer-reviewed journals, including The Historical Journal, Studies in Gothic Fiction, and Journal of Popular Romance Studies. Her books include *Blood Will Tell: A medical explanation for the tyranny of Henry VIII*, and *The Jezebel Effect: Why the slut shaming of famous queens still matters.*

For more information or to contact the author, you can check out her website, kyrackramer.com or her public page on Facebook.

In **Mary Boleyn in a Nutshell**, **Sarah Bryson** discusses the controversies surrounding Mary Boleyn's birth, her alleged relationships with two kings, her portraiture and appearance, and her life and death. Mary survived the brutal events of 1536 and was able to make her own choices, defying the social rules of her times by marrying for love. It is from Mary that the Boleyn bloodline extends to the present day.

Thomas Cranmer

in a nutshell

ISBN: 978-84-943721-3-1

History "In a Nutshell" Series

BETH VON STAATS

In **Thomas Cranmer in a Nutshell**, **Beth von Staats** discusses the fascinating life of **Thomas Cranmer**, from his early education, through his appointment to Archbishop of Canterbury, his growth in confidence as a reformer, the writing of two versions of the English Book of Common Prayer and eventually to his imprisonment, recantations and execution.

Catherine Carey

in a nutshell

ISBN: 978-84-944574-0-1

History "In a Nutshell" Series

ADRIENNE DILLARD

Catherine Carey in a Nutshell examines the life of Catherine Carey, daughter of Mary Boleyn, from the controversy surrounding her paternity through her service to Henry VIII's queens, the trials of life in Protestant exile during the Tudor era, and the triumphant return of the Knollys family to the glittering court of the Virgin Queen. This book brings together what is known about one of Queen Elizabeth I's most trusted and devoted ladies for the first time in one concise, easy-to-read book.

ISBN: 978-15-009962-2-2

CLAIRE RIDGWAY

In **Sweating Sickness in a Nutshell**, **Claire Ridgway** examines what the historical sources say about the five epidemics of the mystery disease which hit England between 1485 and 1551, and considers the symptoms, who it affected, the treatments, theories regarding its cause and why it only affected English people.

MadeGlobal Publishing

Non Fiction History

- Jasper Tudor - **Debra Bayani**
- Tudor Places of Great Britain - **Claire Ridgway**
- Illustrated Kings and Queens of England - **Claire Ridgway**
- A History of the English Monarchy - **Gareth Russell**
- The Fall of Anne Boleyn - **Claire Ridgway**
- George Boleyn: Tudor Poet, Courtier & Diplomat
  - **Ridgway & Cherry**
- The Anne Boleyn Collection - **Claire Ridgway**
- The Anne Boleyn Collection II - **Claire Ridgway**
- Two Gentleman Poets at the Court of Henry VIII
  - **Edmond Bapst**
- A Mountain Road - **Douglas Weddell Thompson**

"History in a Nutshell Series"

- Sweating Sickness in a Nutshell - **Claire Ridgway**
- Mary Boleyn in a Nutshell - **Sarah Bryson**
- Thomas Cranmer in a Nutshell - **Beth von Staats**
- Henry VIII's Health in a Nutshell - **Kyra Kramer**
- Catherine Carey in a Nutshell - **Adrienne Dillard**

Historical Fiction

- Between Two Kings: A Novel of Anne Boleyn - **Olga Lyakina**
- Phoenix Rising - **Hunter S. Jones**
- Cor Rotto - **Adrienne Dillard**
- The Claimant - **Simon Anderson**
- The Truth of the Line - **Melanie V. Taylor**

PLEASE LEAVE A REVIEW

If you enjoyed this book, *please* leave a review at the book seller where you purchased it. There is no better way to thank the author and it really does make a huge difference! *Thank you in advance.*

Lightning Source UK Ltd.
Milton Keynes UK
UKOW06f1953170316

270365UK00007B/53/P